Erin Kissane

W9-BCA-556

THE ELEMENTS OF
CONTENT STRATEGY

Publisher: Jeffrey Zeldman
Designer: Jason Santa Maria
Editor: Mandy Brown
Copyeditor: Krista Stevens

ISBN 978-0-9844425-5-3

A Book Apart
New York, New York
http://books.alistapart.com

10 9 8 7 6 5 4 3 2 1

TABLE OF CONTENTS

FOREWORD

As you can see, the scourge is upon us, and we must, every one of us, be prepared to fight.

—ERIN KISSANE, "Attack of the Zombie Copy"

CONTENT IS A HAIRY, complicated beast. There's stuff to research, sift through, create, curate, correct, schedule—and that's before we start to think about publishing. What layout makes the most sense for this content? What organization? What metaschema? What platforms? Never mind post-launch plans, or lack of resources, or stakeholder alignment, or, or...yikes. No wonder we want to hide under the bed.

The content beast does not scare Erin Kissane. In fact, for her entire adult life, she's been quietly taming it with a firm but gentle hand. As part of her hero's journey, Kissane has collaborated with countless designers, developers, UXers, marketers, editors, and writers on projects of all sizes. This is good news for you: no matter what role you play, she gets what you do and knows why it's important. And, because she cares, she wants to help you understand how content strategy can help make your life a little easier—and your end products a little more awesome.

Not that long ago, I wrote an article that called upon readers to "take up the torch for content strategy." The book you hold in your hands is that torch. So run with it. Hold it high. Be confident in your pursuit of better content. You have *The Elements of Content Strategy* to light your way.

Come on out from under the bed. We have work to do.

—**Kristina Halvorson**
Author, *Content Strategy for the Web*
CEO, Brain Traffic

INTRODUCTION

" Content strategy is to copywriting as information architecture is to design."
—RACHEL LOVINGER

" Content strategy plans for the creation, publication, and governance of useful, usable content."
—KRISTINA HALVORSON

IN THE WEB INDUSTRY, anything that conveys meaningful information to humans is called "content."

Every website has content. Companies with three-page websites probably only need a writer. But those with hundreds or thousands of pieces of online content need someone who can stand back and figure out what all that content should communicate. They also need someone to decide how best to communicate it, who should make it, and so on—a sort of combination editor-in-chief and air traffic controller. They need a content strategist.

In the last few years, the value of content strategy has been articulated in dozens of blog posts, articles, and books, but it's quite simple and worth repeating. Done well, content strategy:

- Helps companies understand and produce the kind of content their target audiences really need.
- Allows organizations to develop realistic, sustainable, and measurable publishing plans that keep their content on track in the long term.
- Cuts costs by reducing redundant or extraneous publishing efforts, while increasing the effectiveness of existing assets.
- Aligns communication across channels so that web content, print collateral, social media conversations, and internal knowledge management are working toward the same goals (in channel-appropriate ways).

- Prevents web projects from being derailed by the often major delays caused by underestimating the time and effort required to produce great content.

And this is only the beginning. Our discipline is in its infancy, and we've had only the tiniest peek at the internet's full impact on the way we live and do business. Content strategy is rising because organizations all over the world have begun to realize that they desperately need it to handle their rapidly expanding online communications. Unless the planet gets hit by a comet, this trend is unlikely to reverse.

What's in this book

This book is not an argument for the importance of content strategy. Neither is it a tutorial, a workbook, or a gallery of deliverables. It will not show you how to turn your BA in English into a $100,000 salary in ten easy steps. And it is emphatically not an exhaustive compendium of everything we know about content work. Instead it collects our discipline's core principles, competencies, and practices for easy reference, divided into three sections:

- "Basic Principles" lays out our discipline's shared values.
- "The Craft of Content Strategy" explores the collected expertise of the fields that have contributed the most to our work.
- "Tools and Techniques" provides a brisk walkthrough of approaches, methods, and deliverables used in the daily practice of content strategy.

You might think of these pieces as a (very) brief handbook, an introduction to a panel of potential mentors, and the key to the supply cabinet. Begin wherever you wish and end where you please. In the back of the book are additional examples and resources. When you're done here, please join the raucous online content conversation, if you haven't already.

When I get stuck on a project or intimidated by a blank page, there are a handful of books I reach for to remind myself what my options are: what else to try, what criteria I should use to judge my work, and how I might think differently about the obstacles ahead. If this book can be such a reference for some of you, I'll consider it a great success.

Onward.

BASIC PRINCIPLES

IN CONTENT STRATEGY, there is no playbook of generic strategies you can pick from to assemble a plan for your client or project. Instead, our discipline rests on a series of core principles about what makes content effective—what makes it work, what makes it good. The first section of this book is organized around these fundamentals.

GOOD CONTENT IS APPROPRIATE

Publish content that is right for the user and for the business

There's really only one central principle of good content: it should be appropriate for your business, for your users, and for its context. Appropriate in its method of delivery, in its style and structure, and above all in its substance. Content strategy is the practice of determining what each of those things means for your project—and how to get there from where you are now.

Right for the user (and context)

Let us meditate for a moment on James Bond. Clever and tough as he is, he'd be mincemeat a hundred times over if not for the hyper-competent support team that stands behind him. When he needs to chase a villain, the team summons an Aston Martin DB5. When he's poisoned by a beautiful woman with dubious connections, the team offers the antidote in a spring-loaded, space-age infusion device. When he emerges from a swamp overrun with trained alligators, it offers a shower, a shave, and a perfectly tailored suit. It does not talk down to him or waste his time. It anticipates his needs, but does not offer him everything he might ever need, all the time.

Content is appropriate for users when it helps them accomplish their goals.

Content is *perfectly* appropriate for users when it makes them feel like geniuses on critically important missions, offering them precisely what they need, exactly when they need it, and in just the right form. All of this requires that you get pretty deeply into your users' heads, if not their tailoring specifications.

Part of this mind-reading act involves context, which encompasses quite a lot more than just access methods, or even a fine-grained understanding of user goals. Content strategist Daniel Eizans has suggested that a meaningful analysis of a user's context requires not only an understanding of users' goals, but also of their behaviors: What are they doing? How are they feeling? What are they capable of? (FIG 1)

It's a sensible notion. When I call the emergency room on a weekend, my context is likely to be quite different than when I call my allergy specialist during business hours. If I look at a subway map at 3:00am, chances are that I need to know which trains are running now, not during rush hour tomorrow. When I look up your company on my phone, I'm more likely to need basic contact info than your annual report from 2006. But assumptions about reader context—however well researched—will never be perfect. Always give readers the option of seeing more information if they wish to do so.

[handwritten margin notes: Content ≠ James Bond analogy. Good content helps users accomplish their goals.]

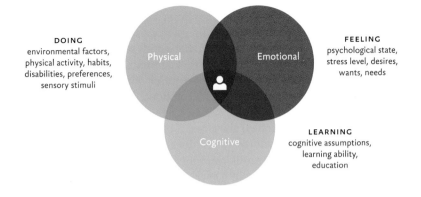

DOING
environmental factors,
physical activity, habits,
disabilities, preferences,
sensory stimuli

FEELING
psychological state,
stress level, desires,
wants, needs

LEARNING
cognitive assumptions,
learning ability,
education

Physical

Emotional

Cognitive

FIG 1: The user's context includes actions, constraints, emotions, cognitive conditions, and more. And that in turn affects the ways in which the user interacts with content. ("Personal-Behavioral Context: The New User Persona." © Daniel Eizans, 2010. Modified from a diagram by Andrew Hinton. http://bkaprt.com/cs/1/)[1]

Right for the business

Content is appropriate for your business when it helps you accomplish your business goals in a sustainable way.

Business goals include things like "increase sales," "improve technical support service," and "reduce printing costs for educational materials," and the trick is to accomplish those goals using sustainable processes. Sustainable content is content you can create—and maintain—without going broke, without lowering quality in ways that make the content suck, and without working employees into nervous breakdowns. The need for this kind of sustainability may sound boneheadedly obvious, but it's very easy to create an ambitious plan for publishing oodles of content without considering the long-term effort required to manage it.

Fundamentally, though, "right for the business" and "right for the user" are the same thing. Without readers, viewers, and listeners, all content is meaningless, and content created without consideration for users' needs harms publishers because ignored users leave.

Enlightened self-interest: that which hurts your users hurts you!

This principle boils down to enlightened self interest: that which hurts your users hurts you.

GOOD CONTENT IS USEFUL

Define a clear, specific purpose for each piece of content; evaluate content against this purpose

Few people set out to produce content that bores, confuses, and irritates users, yet the web is filled with fluffy, purposeless, and annoying content. This sort of content isn't neutral, either: it actively wastes time and money and works against user and business goals.

To know whether or not you have the right content for a page (or module or section), you have to know what that content is supposed to accomplish. Greater specificity produces better results. Consider the following possible purposes for a chunk of product-related content:

- **"Sell products"**—This is so vague as to be meaningless and is likely to produce buzzword-infested fluff.
- **"Sell this product"**—Selling a product is a process made up of many smaller tasks, like discussing benefits, mapping them to features, demonstrating results and value, and asking people to buy. If your goal is this vague, you have no idea which of these tasks (if any) the content will perform.
- **"List and demonstrate the benefits of this product"**—This is something a chunk of content can actually do. But if you don't know who is supposed to benefit from the product, it's difficult to be specific.
- **"Show how this product helps nurse practitioners"**—If you can discover what nurse practitioners need, you can create content that serves this purpose. (And if you *can't* find out what they need before trying to sell them a product, you have a lot more to worry about than your content.)

Now do the same for every chunk of content in your project, and you'll have a useful checklist of what you're really trying to achieve. If that sounds daunting, think how much harder it would be to try to evaluate, create, or revise the content without a purpose in mind.

GOOD CONTENT IS USER-CENTERED

Adopt the cognitive frameworks of your users

On a web project, user-centered design means that the final product must meet real user needs and fulfill real human desires. In practical terms, it also means that the days of designing a site map to mirror an org chart are over.

In *The Psychology of Everyday Things*, cognitive scientist Donald Norman wrote about the central importance of understanding the user's mental model before designing products. In the user-centered design system he advocates, design should "make sure that (1) the user can figure out what to do, and (2) the user can tell what is going on."[2]

When it comes to content, "user-centered" means that instead of insistently using the client's internal mental models and vocabulary, content must adopt the cognitive frameworks of the user. That includes everything from your users' model of the world to the ways in which they use specific terms and phrases. And that part has taken a little longer to sink in.

Allow me to offer a brief illustrative puppet show.

While hanging your collection of framed portraits of teacup poodles, you realize you need a tack hammer. So you pop down to the hardware store and ask the clerk where to find one. "Tools and Construction-Related Accessories," she says. "Aisle five."

> *"Welcome to the Tools and Construction-Related Accessories department, where you will find many tools for construction and construction-adjacent activities. How can we help you?"*
> *"Hi. Where can I find a tack hammer?"*
> *"Did you mean an Upholstery Hammer (Home Use)?"*
> *"...yes?"*

[handwritten margin notes: Content Must adopt the users' cognitive framework from terms/language to model of the world. (tack-hammer example)]

"Hammers with heads smaller than three inches are the responsibility of the Tools for Home Use Division at the far end of aisle nine."

...

"Welcome to The Home Tool Center! We were established by the merger of the Tools for Home Use Division and the Department of Small Sharp Objects. Would you like to schedule a demonstration?"

"I just need an upholstery hammer. For...the home?"

"Do you require Premium Home Use Upholstery Hammer or Standard Deluxe Home Use Upholstery Hammer?"

"Look, there's a tack hammer right behind your head. That's all I need."

"DIRECTORY ACCESS DENIED. Please return to the front of the store and try your search again!"

Publishing content that is self-absorbed in substance or style alienates readers. Most successful organizations have realized this, yet many sites are still built around internal org charts, clogged with mission statements designed for internal use, and beset by jargon and proprietary names for common ideas.

If you're the only one offering a desirable product or service, you might not see the effects of narcissistic content right away, but someone will eventually come along and eat your lunch by offering the exact same thing in a user-centered way.

[handwritten margin note: Self-absorbed content alienates readers.]

GOOD CONTENT IS CLEAR

Seek clarity in all things

When we say that something is clear, we mean that it works; it communicates; the light gets through. Good content speaks to people in a language they understand and is organized in ways that make it easy to use.

Content strategists usually rely on others—writers, editors, and multimedia specialists—to produce and revise the content that users read, listen to, and watch. On some large projects, we may never meet most of the people involved in content production. But if we want to help them produce genuinely clear content, we can't just make a plan, drop it onto the heads of the writers, and flee the building.

The chapters that follow will discuss ways of creating useful style guides, consulting on publishing workflow, running writing and editorial workshops, and developing tools like content templates, all of which are intended to help content creators produce clear, useful content in the long term.

Of course, clarity is also a virtue we should attend to in the production of our own work. Goals, meetings, deliverables, processes—all benefit from a love of clarity.

GOOD CONTENT IS CONSISTENT

Mandate consistency, within reason

For most people, language is our primary interface with each other and with the external world. Consistency of language and presentation acts as a consistent interface, reducing the users' cognitive load and making it easier for readers to understand what they read. Inconsistency, on the other hand, adds cognitive effort, hinders understanding, and distracts readers.

That's what our style guides are for. Many of us who came to content strategy from journalistic or editorial fields have a very strong attachment to a particular style—I have a weakness for the *Chicago Manual of Style*—but skillful practitioners put internal consistency well ahead of personal preferences.

Some kinds of consistency aren't always uniformly valuable, either: a site that serves doctors, patients, and insurance providers, for example, will probably use three different voice/tone guidelines for the three audiences, and another for content intended to be read by a general audience. That's healthy, reader-centric consistency. On the other hand, a company that permitted each of its product teams to create widely different kinds of content is probably breaking the principles of consistency for self-serving, rather than reader-serving, reasons.

GOOD CONTENT IS CONCISE

Omit needless content

Some organizations love to publish lots of content. Perhaps because they believe that having an org chart, a mission statement, a vision declaration, and a corporate inspirational video on the About Us page will retroactively validate the hours and days of time spent producing that content. Perhaps because they believe Google will only bless their work if they churn out dozens of blog posts per week. In most cases, I think entropy deserves the blame: the web offers the space to publish everything, and it's much easier to treat it like a hall closet with infinite stuffing-space than to impose constraints.

So what does it matter if we have too much content? For one thing, more content makes everything more difficult to find. For another, spreading finite resources ever more thinly results in a decline in quality. It also often indicates a deeper problem—publishing *everything* often means "publishing everything we can," rather than "publishing everything we've learned that our users really need."

There are many ways to discover which content is in fact needless; traffic analysis, user research, and editorial judgment should all play a role. You may also wish to begin with a hit list of common stowaways:

- **Mission statements, vision statements, and core values.** If the people within your organization are genuinely committed to abstract principles, it will show in what they do. The exception is the small number of organizations for whom the mission is the product, as is the case with many charities. Even then, this kind of content should be supplemented with plentiful evidence of follow-through.
- **Press releases.** These may work for their very narrow intended audience, but putting them undigested onto a website is a perfect example of the how-we've-always-done-it mistake.
- **Long, unreadable legal pages.** Some legal awkwardness is acceptable, but if you want to demonstrate that you respect

your readers, take the extra time to whittle down rambling legalese and replace needless circumlocutions with (attorney-vetted) plain language.

- **Endless feature lists.** Most are not useful to readers. The few that are can usually be organized into subcategories that aid findability and comprehension.
- **Redundant documentation.** Are you offering the same audience three different FAQs? Can they be combined or turned into contextual help?
- **Audiovisual dust bunnies.** Do your videos or animations begin with a long flying-logo intro? Do they ramble on for 30 minutes to communicate ten minutes of important content? Trim, edit, and provide ways of skipping around.

Once you've rooted out unnecessary content at the site-planning level, be prepared to ruthlessly eliminate (and teach others to eliminate) needless content at the section, page, and sentence level.

GOOD CONTENT IS SUPPORTED

Publish no content without a support plan

If newspapers are "dead tree media," information published online is a live green plant. And as we figured out sometime around 10,000 BC, plants are more useful if we tend them and shape their futures to suit our goals. So, too, must content be tended and supported.

Factual content must be updated when new information appears and culled once it's no longer useful; user-generated content must be nurtured and weeded; time-sensitive content like breaking news or event information must be planted on schedule and cut back once its blooming period ends. Perhaps most importantly, a content plan once begun must be carried through its intended growth cycle if it's to bear fruit and make all the effort worthwhile.

This is all easy to talk about, but the reason most content is not properly maintained is that most content plans rely on getting the already overworked to produce, revise, and publish content without neglecting other responsibilities. This is not inevitable, but unless content and publishing tasks are recognized as time-consuming and complex and then included in job descriptions, performance reviews, and resource planning, it will continue.

Hoping that a content management system will replace this kind of human care and attention is about as effective as pointing a barn full of unmanned agricultural machinery at a field, going on vacation, and hoping it all works out. Tractors are more efficient than horse-drawn plows, but they still need humans to decide where and when and how to use them.

No matter how we come to content strategy, or what kind of content strategy work we do, these shared principles and assumptions underlie our work. Of course, these principles didn't emerge from a vacuum. Content strategy is a young field, but it has evolved from professions that are anything but new. To understand the full scope of what content strategy can do—and to understand why it isn't "just editing" or "another word for marketing," let's take a look at the professions that have laid the groundwork for our practice.

---

1. The long URL: http://www.slideshare.net/danieleizans/context-as-a-content-strategy-creating-more-meaningful-web-experiences-through-contextual-filtering
2. Donald Norman, *The Psychology of Everyday Things*, (New York: Basic Books, 1988), 188.

THE CRAFT OF CONTENT STRATEGY

BECAUSE CONTENT has so frequently demonstrated its potential to derail web projects, and because it is uniquely entangled with business strategy, it requires special attention. Throughout each project, a content strategist compares evolving content-related expectations with available resources, and warns the team of shortfalls that may require that the content work be scaled back or the resources stepped up. She navigates the politically fraught territory of distributed publishing, and long after information architecture and visual design work is approved, she keeps an eye on the ways in which organizational strategy changes affect ongoing content work.

In short, she watches the hills for signs of trouble.

To do content strategy, defined as the planning and leadership of content projects and online publishing endeavors, is to run point. The term "run point" derives from a military term for the soldier or soldiers who moved ahead of the rest of the advancing troops: the point man. An equally influential and appropriate use in American English refers to the cowboy who rides at the front of a herd of cattle. The current version of Wikipedia article for "Take Point" notes in characteristically deadpan prose that "It is a hazardous position that requires alertness and ability to deal with unexpected attacks" (http://bkaprt.com/cs/2/).[1] Indeed.

In her role as point man, a content strategist works with other front-runners who lead various aspects of the project: information architects, technical leads, creative directors, and project managers. And in addition to leading content work, she plays a key role in what business consultants call "risk management." Paradoxically, if your content strategist spots a problem late in a project and takes a hit—either by doing extra work or mandating a brief delay—that means the process is working. If someone's going to hit a snag, you *want* it to be your content strategist, not the content creators or an SEO specialist or the person in charge of a database migration.

So naturally, if you're the one doing content strategy, you need to be able to sniff out trouble and react quickly when it does arise. One of the best ways to prepare yourself for upcoming challenges is to push yourself beyond the boundaries of the field you came from. And that means learning about the other fields from which content strategy descends.

A tangled family tree

Marketers tend to characterize content strategy as a form of marketing—as do some technical communicators, though the latter group means it as an insult. Knowledge management people often say it's a way of improving processes and setting standards. Longtime web editors and writers tend to assume that it's what they've been doing all along. None of them are dead wrong, but neither are they completely right. And as the definitional debates rage on, it's increasingly clear that our discipline is vulnerable to being co-opted by nearby fields, or to being distorted by the fact that online, some of those fields are much louder and more public than others.

That's why we need to know our roots. If you know who you are—and how you got that way—it's going to be much harder for someone else to define you into a corner. Not to mention that if you know at least some of the tricks and traditions and history of your tribe, you won't have to reinvent it all by yourself.

The origin of the species

It's nice to think of our field as a vigorous hybrid, but it often feels more like a Frankenstein's monster assembled from spare parts and animated by deadline-inspired panic. Also appropriate: the ancient Greek creature called the Chimera, a fire-breathing monster with the head of a lion on one end, the head of a serpent on the other, and a goat's head growing out of the middle of its body. (I'll just let you think about that for a minute.)

Designers have a pantheon they can point to: Paula Scher and Saul Bass, but also Bodoni and Gutenberg. Developers have cultural heroes like Alan Turing and Sir Tim Berners-Lee. These disciplines have legacies and shared principles. *Design should communicate. Elegant code is better than sloppy code.*

Though it lacks a goat head, content strategy also has a legacy. Several, in fact. And each has plenty to teach us. A complete genetic breakdown would require a separate book, so for now, let's consider the four most influential fields: editorial work, curatorial work, marketing and persuasion, and information science.

INFLUENCE #1: THE EDITOR

Editorial work is so closely related to content strategy that questions about the difference between the two often arise. From the outside, content strategy can look quite a lot like the sort of editing found in magazines and newspapers. The editorial world, and that of publishing in general, has a lot to offer us.

For people outside of the publishing industry, the title of editor may raise the specter of the cranky, scotch-drinking, overcoat-wearing, borderline dysfunctional editors played by the likes of Humphrey Bogart and Cary Grant. Alternatively, those traumatized as children by English teachers may expect an editor to pride herself on being a "stickler" and whack you on the knuckles when you split an infinitive.

It's true that an ear for correct language is helpful and that a passion for getting the story told right is indispensable. But real-world editing is much more about crack organizational skills, a habit of developing practical communication ideas, and the ability to deal firmly and diplomatically with the whole crew of people involved in getting a book, newspaper, or website from concept to delivery. Editors don't just assign stories and make margin notes in blue pencil: they develop themes and narrative arcs, orchestrate responses to other publications and outside events, maintain a balanced variety of articles or books, evaluate and manage writers and other content creators, and much more.

Leaving aside the knuckle-whacking, editors have plenty to teach us about handling content.

Content people work for the user

In publishing, if you don't win, hold, and reward the attention of your readers—whether they're fans of tabloid journalism or wistful MFA-program novels—you're out of a job. Editors worth their salt work not for writers or publishers, but for readers.

Editors work for Readers.

Though content specialists must often mediate between product teams, marketing and corporate communication departments, special initiatives, and development staff, we too work for readers. In *Content Strategy for the Web*, Kristina Halvorson writes:[2]

> ...online, you don't have a captive audience. You have a multi-tasking, distracted, ready-to-leave-your-site-at-any-time audience who has very specific goals in mind.
> If your content doesn't meet those goals, and quickly, they will leave.

Online users have specific goals. If you don't meet them, they'll leave.

This fact—that the reader's interest and attention is the central, precious thing—is the professional editor's mantra. Here's one of my favorite passages from Arthur Plotnik's wonderful *The Elements of Editing*:[3]

> *An editor's only permanent alliance is with the audience, the readership. It is the editor's responsibility to hook that readership; to edify it, entertain it, stroke it, shake it up...Authors know their subject. Editors specialize in knowing the audience.*

YES!

Great writers know what their readers want and need to hear. But the responsibility for validating assumptions about the audience and tuning the content to suit that audience remains with the editors—and now the content strategists—of the world. Paradoxically, it's only by working tirelessly for our readers that we can genuinely serve our clients and employers.

Stories matter

Humans are compulsive storytellers. We think and teach and connect by creating stories. And the thinkers who change opinions, the teachers who inspire students, the politicians who win elections, and of course, the publishers who sell books and magazines all tend to have something in common: they can tell a great story.

For anyone who communicates as a profession, stories are the ultimate hack.

Whatever corner of the publishing world they come from, editors know how to help other people tell the best, most engaging stories they can tell. Content people with backgrounds in journalism or publishing usually have the basics of storytelling down cold, but the rest of us can learn from the storytelling principles of these fields—from the basics like building a lead that hooks the reader (and supporting it with facts and quotations) to sophisticated techniques for layering in secondary narratives.

If you're not entirely comfortable with your understanding of storytelling, it can be helpful to go back to the elementary principles taught in high-school journalism classes—familiar concepts like:

- **The inverted pyramid:** This term describes a classic news story structure in which all the most important basic information appears at the beginning of the story, and is followed by less important information ordered from most important to least important.
  "Important" here means important to the reader. Note that this is the exact opposite of the fluffiest sort of marketing copy that begins with statements like "The world of international business is getting ever more complicated."
- **5 Ws and an H:** You may remember this one from grade school. It's intended to remind writers that they need to explain the basics of every story: what happened, who is involved, when and where it happened, why it happened, and how it happened. If you happen to be writing marketing copy, this might translate to what the product is, who it's made for, why the intended audience should buy it, how it works, and when and where you can get it.
- **Show, don't tell:** Instead of going on and on about how wonderful and leading-edge your widget is or how much your client cherishes its mission statement, give evidence. Show results, statistics, case studies, personal narratives, and demonstrations of action, and give the puffery a rest.

Of course, these principles are mere starting points. Storytelling isn't something you learn from a list of tips or a podcast about narrative tricks. You *can* learn a lot by analyzing structure and practicing technique, but you also have to dig in and read, watch, and listen to the great stories being spun by novelists, journalists, screenwriters, and—yes—bloggers and marketers. (This will make you not only a better content strategist, but also a more interesting dinner companion.)

But why bother with all that if you're not going to be creating the content yourself? Primarily, because most content strategy projects deal with narratives: brand messages, overarching themes, and communication plans all center on the reader's progression through a series of ideas. And secondarily, because if you're going to design guidelines and processes for content creators, you need to understand narrative well enough to give them the right tools for telling strong stories.

Finally, a word on working with storytellers.

One of the spookiest aspects of the editorial craft is the ability to nudge, cajole, or otherwise wrangle each author into producing his or her best work *without* diluting the individual author's voice and perspective. It's tricky as hell and requires an ever-shifting balance of tact and frankness. Whenever you approach content creators, it's worth spending a little extra effort on communicating with them in ways that neither devastate nor condescend.

Publishing is hard

In the brief history of the internet so far, two kinds of content-related train wrecks stand out:

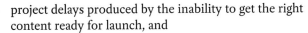

Why Content Is So Critical to Consider!

- project delays produced by the inability to get the right content ready for launch, and
- project derailments caused by a lack of planning for ongoing content oversight, production, revision, and distribution—what Jeffrey MacIntyre of Predicate, LLC, aptly calls "The Day Two Problem" (http://bkaprt.com/cs/3/)[4].

Both problems are caused by underestimating the time, attention, skill, and money required to plan, create, and publish content, both immediately and in the long term. As a species, we've been doing all that since about 2000 BC, so we happen to know quite a lot about it. But before the internet, the vast majority of people who had to worry about the nuances of publishing were...publishers.

Now that organizations ranging from hospitals and libraries to boutiques and family vineyards have all learned that doing business online involves dealing with content, the gritty details of the publishing process have become relevant to a much wider group. If you need to produce useful, high-quality content at any level beyond the personal weblog, you need an editorial process that will support creation, review and revision, publication, performance tracking, and ongoing maintenance. (You're also going to need resources, primarily in the form of time, which gets paid for with money.)

As content strategists, we can help our teams and clients communicate more effectively by introducing common tools of the publishing trade. Tools such as:

- **clearly documented editorial workflows**, including approval processes and thorough quality checks;
- **editorial calendars** including content campaigns and themes planned well in advance; and
- **content custom-tuned for specific channels and audiences**.

Most importantly, editors can teach us quite a lot about how to regularly publish original content that readers can use. In part, they can demonstrate how to hire and manage writers who can listen to experts, and then collect and create content that extends well beyond executive bios and annual reports.

Our clients and employers are beginning to understand that they need to do more than simply hire a web writer at the end of a project and hope someone else will maintain the content later. As their content specialists, the more we know about solid editorial practices, the better we can help our clients with the transition to the new world of distributed online publishing.

Content is expensive

Useful content is expensive. This is a fact that editors have long understood, but web companies have only just begun to discover.

Leaving aside the effort required to publish a daily newspaper, consider just the people involved in book publishing: the acquisition editors, development editors, copyeditors, proofreaders, book designers, compositors, project managers, cover designers, and sales and marketing teams. In traditional publishing, these people are paid. As are the accountants, secretaries, printers, and everyone else who isn't an intern.

Now consider the marketing lead who receives word that he must now review and revise forty pages of content inherited from another department, ensure that new brand guidelines are implemented in all newsletters and emails, and produce an episode of the company's new video series. In the next three weeks, with no budget increase, and without ditching other responsibilities.

Content strategy recommendations made without consideration of available resources are unlikely to result in success. When we work with big organizations, we may be able to simply note that our recommendations will require additional resources to execute. With smaller companies, we can't simply assume that our clients will magic up an extra twenty hours a week to implement a full-scale "content marketing" plan—or anything else very time-consuming. In some cases, we may have to limit our plans to things that can be accomplished by reshuffling existing staff members and budgets. Whatever the situation, it's our responsibility to:

- **Understand existing resources**: Are there people available to work on content? Are they good at it? What kind of training do they need? Are there other writers or editors in the company who might be made available to help? Is there a budget for hiring freelancers or new staff members?
- **Make the business case for content strategy**: How will the recommended content changes meet overarching organizational goals? Will they replace less efficient processes, and if so, what resources will they free up? Will they directly contribute to revenue increases by boosting sales? Cut costs by reducing customer service hours? Bring in new business by improving the company's brand image?
- **Prepare clients and managers for organizational change**: Can we begin introducing new systems and processes well in advance of publication deadlines? If new people will be hired, can we help with job descriptions or make

hiring recommendations? Can we refer talented, reliable freelancers?

At the end of the day, we and our clients must remember than content is created (and revised and maintained) only when a human being is assigned and paid to do so.
The notion that content is expensive brings up another topic as well, though it's one this book lacks the space to address. Within the field of content strategy, a sub-specialization dedicated to the *business* side of large-scale content production and distribution has begun to emerge. Although many organizations produce content under the aegis of marketing or fundraising, some are in the business of content itself. Publishers qualify, of course, but so does the sprawling beast we call the entertainment industry and the many new kinds of companies that have sprung up to take advantage of the internet's ultra-cheap distribution model. Content specialists who have a talent for financial strategy and the nerve to experiment will likely find this niche both interesting and lucrative.

INFLUENCE #2: THE CURATOR

The word "curator" comes from the Latin "cura," meaning care. The original curators cared for public resources in ancient Rome: grain and oil supplies, aqueducts, public account books, and roads all had their own curators. In fourteenth-century England, the term came to refer to Christian clerics whose primary responsibility was the spiritual cure or care of their parishioners. In the 1660s, we finally begin to see the word begin to refer to "the officer in charge of a museum, gallery of art, library, or the like; a keeper, custodian" (http://bkaprt.com/cs/4/).[5]
In a consideration of this evolution, art-world critic David Levi Strauss writes that curators "have always been a curious mixture of bureaucrat and priest" (http://bkaprt.com/cs/5/),[6] balancing practical administration with the care of the soul. And as content strategist Dan Zambonini has written, these

museum and gallery curators care *for*—rather than merely *about*—their collections (http://bkaprt.com/cs/6/).[7]

And this gets to the heart of our work as content strategists. We must plan for the orderly acquisition, cataloging, and practical maintenance of the content in our care. But just as much, we must protect its essence and truthfulness, and keep it safe from creeping degradation of quality and tone. In both of these contexts, curators can offer useful tools, frameworks, and lessons.

Immersion matters

In a 2006 interview, the late Anne d'Harnoncourt, director of the Philadelphia Museum of Art for twenty-six years and daughter of famous curator and museum director René d'Harnoncourt, was asked for a word of advice to young curators. Her advice was "to look and look and look, and then to look again, because nothing replaces looking...to *be* with art."[8]

Most of the content that most of us work with (most of the time) is not art. But the curatorial notion of consciously *being* with art—what critic Michael Fried calls "presentness"—is doubly relevant to our work.[9]

In one sense, it can refer to our own immersion in the content we work with—our pursuit of a knowledge that goes beyond simple familiarity. In the same interview mentioned above, d'Harnoncourt discussed her father's groundbreaking 1939 exhibition of Native American art at the World's Fair in San Francisco. René d'Harnoncourt, she recalls,[10]

> spent years of his life really getting to know the people who made these objects, and so when he presented them, whether it was a sand painting, or totem poles from the north-west coast, or whatever it was, he tried to do...something that really respected the context in which it was made and at the same time would allow it to communicate to an audience not accustomed to seeing these things as the very, very beautiful and powerful things that they were.

The degree of expertise, sensitivity, and good judgment required of prominent curators may seem excessive to the content specialist whose "collections" reside in databases, but this description of a curator's work should be ringing bells. To do our jobs well, we must balance an understanding of the context in which content is created (sourcing, business goals, workflow) with an understanding of the context in which it is read and used (user needs, delivery channels). And immersion in both worlds is what makes the right balance possible.

The second way in which curatorial ideas about presentness and focused attention cross into our discipline is all about the user.

In effective museum and gallery installations, visitors are usually invited to spend time simply being with art—or artifacts or other content. Curators and exhibition designers understand that people require certain things to have concentrated experiences: things like unobstructed access, good light, and freedom from distractions.

Now imagine going into a museum and trying to walk up to a Matisse, only to run into a glass wall ten feet away from the painting. To get past the wall—which is now frosted so you can't see the painting at all—you have to write down your full name and address, and then show ID to prove that you are who you say you are. Once you've submitted to all this, you discover that the "painting" is only a small print— you have to go into another room full of billboards to see the original. Finally, you reach the painting. The descriptive label is written in miniature gray text on a slightly lighter gray background, so forget trying to read that, but here at last is the art.

awesome analogy

That's when the circus clowns pop out of the woodwork and start honking little horns and waving signs advertising tooth-whitening products and diet pills. This is content online.

The fact that anyone reads anything at all online is a demonstration of an extraordinary hunger for content. Leaving aside the distractions of email, other websites, and real life, we have built tens of thousands of websites around the idea

the fact that people are supposed

that no matter how demanding, annoying, and abusive our sites become, our readers will keep coming back for our content. But is this really the best we can do? Of course it isn't. And we should consider it part of our work as content strategists to ensure that all the effort and attention poured into creating and managing great content isn't drowned out by interfaces that obstruct, annoy, and distract.

In a 2009 *A List Apart* article, designer and editor Mandy Brown challenges web designers to create space for readers. Echoing d'Harnoncourt, Brown advises designers that to do so, they must first allow themselves to become absorbed in the text (http://bkaprt.com/cs/7/):[11]

> As a designer, the only way to ensure that the page makes for good reading is to read it yourself; to relinquish the design sensibility that is inclined to look at text and take the time to actually read it. It's not an easy task, but then, neither is reading on the web, and making the effort may help you empathize with the reader's plight. The web is still a noisy, crowded place—but it's also limitless, and surely we can find space enough for reading—a space where the text speaks to the reader and the reader does not strain to hear.

In addition to attending to design considerations like whitespace and typesetting, we can act as user advocates by advising our clients and employers to reduce distractions in sidebars, fight ads that obstruct content, and give readers the equivalent of good light and a quiet room. This is one of the reasons that a multidisciplinary approach can potentially produce better results than content-only gigs for some kinds of projects—when content specialists can weigh in on presentation and design, readers benefit.

Users are people, too

Much of the design and planning work done in major museums and galleries is not theoretical, or even particularly curatorial. Curators and other museum workers deal with physical objects and corporeal humans in real spaces. And those humans, being mammals, need things like places to sit, reasonable ambient temperatures, wheelchair ramps and other accessibility aids, drinking water, and bathrooms. In larger museums, they also need security guards to protect them from each other, friendly staff members who can provide information in several languages, well designed maps, and someplace to get a sandwich and a coffee.

On the web, we deal with each other in heavily mediated ways, but we're all still primates. We need accommodations for the thousand disabilities that we experience; ways of marking and saving information for later so we can take breaks; ways of skipping through content when we're in a hurry; friendly orientation and navigation aids; access to real human assistance, via live help, telephone, email, or any other reasonable channel; and the ability to consume content on the devices and in the locations of our choice.

But aren't these user experience concerns? They are indeed. And as content advocates, we should be ready to contribute to the design of user experiences that involve our content.

In short, we should strive to create and present content in ways that respect the fact that even when they're using the web, people need to pee.   *haha!*

"Painstaking" isn't an insult

Museum and gallery curators often handle priceless, irreplaceable objects. Accordingly, they use formalized and meticulous processes for accepting, describing, and tracking the items they care for. Similar processes, applied to content, can significantly reduce the chaos of large-scale content projects, but they need not stop there.

Most content specialists who lead large projects have learned to institute orderly content-documentation processes well before a new site launch, largely because the alternative is so painful. But although taxonomies and metadata matter quite a lot, it's easy to accidentally omit other potentially important information:

- What information about content sources and types should we record to ease future display, reuse, revision, and expansion?
- When content is added or revised, how can we usefully document the reasons for the change? And how can we ensure that ongoing, distributed revisions fit within a larger communication strategy?
- What processes might let us track and reuse our content resources over time? What kind of reporting, analysis, and publishing tools would such tracking and reuse require? How can we structure our content to promote reuse in interesting ways?
- How might we use analytics and other tools to understand which assets we're under-using?

We'll return to some of these notions in a few pages, but for now, it's worth noting that a curatorial approach to long-term content management crosses over into the domain frequently occupied by IT teams, marketing departments, and the "webmasters" of the past.

INFLUENCE #3: THE MARKETER

Marketing is the practice of bringing products to market and persuading people to buy them. The "products" involved may be literal (eggs, laptops, ebooks) or metaphorical (ideas, experiences, political candidates), and the means may include techniques ranging from the obvious to the extremely subtle. Content strategy is not a subset of marketing, but marketing is one possible application of content strategy, and we derive many common content strategy methods and practices from marketing.

Most of marketing is, in turn, derived from rhetoric: the practice of writing or speaking to persuade. From the moment of its birth, rhetoric has been viewed with a certain amount of suspicion. Back in the fourth century BC, Plato compared rhetoric to the black art of cooking, which makes unhealthy food taste good and thus is (like rhetoric) a kind of deception. (Of course, Plato also suggested that his utopian republic would only succeed if everyone ate and slept on the floor and consumed only bread, nuts, and berries; meat, tables, and beds all led directly to doom.)

This cultural ambivalence about the arts of persuasion is nowhere more clear than in the world of marketing.

Rhetoric and persuasion, whether you want 'em or not

When we create content for businesses and other organizations, we usually need to do more than inform or entertain. In theory, there are exceptions—newspaper sites and so on—but for most businesses and institutions, online content is also intended to intrigue, to persuade, and ultimately, to sell.

Happily, this doesn't mean that websites should be like direct mail. Sometimes "selling" is so subtle as to be nearly invisible, and sometimes it's as straightforward as saying "we made this cool thing that you can use to do great stuff—would you like to buy it?" Mostly, it's somewhere in between. And the principles of persuasion (rhetoric) and selling (marketing) are something that modern western civilization has down cold.

Rhetoric constitutes one of the three parts of the trivium— a big chunk of the old-school classical education—and is also a highly contested field of academic study. I will now oversimplify to the point of cartoonishness.

According to Aristotle, the three kinds of rhetoric are:

- The rational argument (logos). *Our widget will produce these benefits for your company, as you can clearly see from this table of research data which I have printed in six-point type. Ta-da!*
- The emotional appeal (pathos). *Happy memories are the most precious things in our brief, sad lives. Won't you buy this widget to make you some happy memories?*
- The appeal grounded in the speaker's reputation or character (ethos). *As a thought leader in the fields of both thought and leadership, I tell you: Buy this widget. You won't regret it.*

The principles of rhetoric are embedded in our culture of communication, appearing not only in marketing, but opinion columns, blogs, and, of course, political speeches—the latter being the original rhetoric, from the world's original democracy.

In the language of marketers, "messages" are very high-level ideas you want to transmit directly into your users' brains, and they're created by combining *what* you need to say with a rhetorical approach—*how* you need to say it. These messages aren't taglines; they're for internal use and will act as scaffolding for your content, supporting and shaping the content you actually produce. (You may also hear them called "messaging," but let's avoid that invitation to the grammar smackdown.) *lol,*

To see how this plays out, consider the messages that a flower shop in Brooklyn, an upscale hotel catering to business travelers, and a state university might assemble (if they were a little punchy and over-caffeinated) (TABLE 1).

In most cases, at least some brand messages will have been handed down from an internal marketing group. And remember, if you're working on content strategy and you've been given only top-level messages, you're well within your rights to push for more specific messages to help you shape your content. In fact, doing otherwise would be a mistake.

There's a whole lot more to rhetoric than this tiny nibble can convey, and it's a field begging to be examined by content specialists of all kinds. Content consultant Colleen Jones puts it this way (http://bkaprt.com/cs/8/):[12]

Rhetoric is the study of using language to persuade or influence. It's been around since Aristotle. How can we ignore rhetoric— the persuasive use of words—as we try to make our word-filled websites persuasive? That would be like trying to bake a delicious cake with no understanding of flour, milk, or chocolate.

Crimes against cake are not to be ignored, and neither is the rich tradition of rhetoric. And if the modern language of marketing makes you twitchy, a good dose of rhetorical theory may be just what you need to get your brain in gear and create persuasive content. (If this subject interests you, get thee to a copy of *Clout*, by Colleen Jones. It's a superb resource for content people, whether or not they're in marketing, and it has

CLIENT	CORE IDEA	RATIONAL APPEAL	EMOTIONAL APPEAL	REPUTATION-BASED APPEAL
Local florist	Our flowers are the freshest.	Our flowers last 30% longer and are more beautiful because they're so fresh.	Vibrantly fresh flowers will make your life feel beautiful.	Our family has been in the floral business for 100 years. We know from fresh.
Business hotel	We're less hassle than other hotels.	Choose us and you will spend less time during registration and checkout. Guaranteed.	From the moment you walk in the door, you're in your own personal office—or private executive lounge.	We've served more traveling executives than anyone else, so we understand what business travelers need.
State university	Our academic programs are strong.	Most of our programs are ranked in the US News and World Report Top 25, and 70% of our graduates go on to pursue master's or doctoral degrees.	Apply here to study with the most inspiring professors this side of Hogwarts.	We are the most selective state university in the US, and our faculty offers an unparalleled reputation for excellence in their fields.

TABLE 1: The three major kinds of rhetorical appeal as applied to hypothetical client situations.

an entire chapter on rhetoric that is vastly more sophisticated than my comic-book overview.)

Evaluation rocks

Marketing people—and especially their advertising brethren—succeed when they persuade their target audiences to act in a particular way. In other words, they can measure success by measuring how many new desired actions they've inspired. In the print world, this has long been a sticky problem. If you run shampoo commercials on television while also putting ads in magazines and on the sides of city buses, how will you know which part of your campaign is helping the most? This problem is why marketers invented coupons and discount codes—they're trackable.

On the internet, things are different and just about everything ad-viewers and other web users do can be tracked and analyzed. In the last 15 years, marketers have made a science of online performance analysis, and there's an intimidatingly large body of literature (well, maybe "literature") on the subject, about which more in Chapter 3. For now, consider this: if you're going to work with content on the internet, you need to make and execute a solid plan for determining whether or not what you do works.

If you're coming to content strategy without a marketing background, it may be hard to tell the broad, genuinely useful approaches from the Google-Ad-Your-Way-To-Success stuff. I quite like Eric T. Peterson's *Web Analytics Demystified* and *The Big Book of Key Performance Indicators*, which take a more holistic approach to performance measurement than most books that focus exclusively on hit counts and click-tracking. Both books are out of print, *but* both are available as free downloads from the author's website (http://bkaprt.com/cs/9/).[13]

Channels differ

In the marketing world, "delivery channels" used to mean "ways of distributing actual products." Now it means about six different things, so let's be clear. When I say "distribution channel" and "channel strategy," I'm talking about the method of getting content to its intended audience. Methods like:

- "The website"—what you think of when you imagine a corporation's main website
- Sites aimed at subsets of the main audience (microsites, topical sites) or specific regions (often in translation or with content created for local audiences)
- Blogs, whether or not they live within another site
- Newsletters
- Social communication channels (Facebook, Twitter, and their hundred million friends)
- Webcasts, podcasts, and video series
- Online magazines
- Mobile applications
- Third-party applications, publications, and sites
- Downloadable text-based content like whitepapers, ebooks, and special reports

And channel strategy? That's the part where you use all the things you've learned about your users and your business goals to figure out the best way of getting your content to your humans. Marketing people have been thinking about this for a long time, and have a lot to teach about it.

Note: You may have noticed that I don't really talk about "web content" in this book. That's because the web is just one piece of the online content world, and "web" vs. "not web" isn't an especially useful way to think about distribution. "We'll put it on the web" isn't a very helpful distribution plan—much less useful than "this would be a good thing to summarize in the blog, publish as a full-length article on an external website, and mention in our newsletter and social media channels," or "this piece can be a video podcast, with segment-specific cross-promotion on other channels."

INFLUENCE #4: THE (INFO) SCIENTIST

Information scientists come in many flavors. Some of them are librarians, archivists, data analysts, informaticians, digital curators, and other info-slingers with a very wide range of titles. They have one thing in common, which is that they work on ways of effectively storing, retrieving, and disseminating information.

If your native approach comes from editorial or marketing work, prop your eyelids open, because this matters for you. Here's why: information science gave us much of what has turned into the modern practice of information architecture, which is what saves our slaved-over and expensive content from dissolving into a formless puddle of goo.

Information architecture

Information architecture is the design of structures for information, including navigational structures and content taxonomies. The people who do this work strive to bring order to chaos and build structures that help users find what they're looking for and accomplish the tasks they set out to do. They create marvelous items like wireframes, site maps, page diagrams, and user flows, and often also do enormous amounts of user research beforehand.

If you're working with an information architect, you may not need to concern yourself with the details of structural design except in areas where content strategy and information architecture overlap. Navigation labels and taxonomies are one obvious conjunction, particularly for content strategists with an editorial background. Detailed wireframes can bring together structural thinking with actual content—or at least, very good example content—long before visual design begins, thus giving both the information architect and the content strategist time to discover gaps and potential conflicts. Beyond specific deliverables, though, even more interesting collaborations are possible. Design often requires input from content people and programmers as well as information architects; content management system specifications can likewise benefit from this input.

Of course, if you're not working with an IA, but you are involved in a serious site-building or redesign project, you may have to be the IA as well as the content specialist. And while

 A BOOK APART

Dear Reader—

Back in the web's Pleistocene period, I received an email from a young content strategist. "Excuse me," she wrote, "but there is a grammatical error in the current issue of *A List Apart*." While I was used to reader mail challenging the ideas in our articles, it was the first time anybody had bothered themselves about the writing. "Would you like to be my copyeditor?" I shot back.

Within months, Erin had worked her way up to editor-in-chief. For ten years, she supervised the magazine's strategic growth, fostered its embrace of multiple disciplines, and interacted skillfully and graciously with the leading minds in web design—our writers. Simultaneously with her editorial work, Erin helped pioneer content strategy for clients large and small, working closely with editors, curators, designers, developers, marketers, you name it. She learned enough about everyone's jobs to value what they do, get the information great content strategy requires, and sell content strategy to them—for, like everything else in this business, persuasion is at least half the job.

At last, in this book, she shares what she knows. In the past, only her friends, clients, and lucky writers got to know the magic that is Erin Kissane. Now she belongs to everybody. Read this book, enjoy it (Erin is a hell of a writer), and go make the web better.

Yours,
Jeffrey Zeldman

| Jeffrey Zeldman | Jason Santa Maria | Mandy Brown |
| *Publisher* | *Designer* | *Editor* |

it takes years of hard work and scads of hours spent in deep thought to get really good at information architecture—or anything else worth doing—you can start using the techniques and tools of information architecture almost immediately. User proxies like personas and scenarios can be tremendously helpful even if they're scribbled in crayon, as long as they're grounded in research and based on reasonable assumptions. Even rudimentary wireframes can save an IA-less project from falling into chaos, and all content strategists can benefit from a solid understanding of the principles of usability and findability, both of which are essential to information architecture.

Content management

You know how websites all used to be made of individual, hard-coded HTML pages? That sucked.

If you weren't around for that part of the web, think of it as the scribes-in-monasteries period of web history during which all written human knowledge was hand-copied by very pale guys with poor eyesight. The invention of the web has been compared to Gutenberg's introduction of movable type, and for good reason—but on the web content side, our communication revolution really took place when software developers brought the database-and-display-template systems of the old offline computing world onto the web in the form of content management systems.

The first major content management systems were the lumbering and expensive descendents of old-school document-management systems. So corporate and institutional content managers (mostly known as "webmasters" at that point) were the first ones to break out into the daylight of content management. All the content that had been tortured into blocks of HTML was suddenly given a home in a database, which meant that "revising the boilerplate" suddenly meant making copy changes in one or two places, instead of five or ten. Site redesigns began to seem just hard instead of utterly impossible.

Eventually, both blogging software and open-source content management systems emerged, and while the former got more sophisticated, the latter got easier and easier to use until the two were indistinguishable. Anyone with basic computer skills could publish content online, and major online publishers could do their work more efficiently and for less money. As of 2010, WordPress, the most popular blogging-application-turned-CMS, has nearly 30 million users worldwide and powers approximately 12% of all websites (http://bkaprt.com/cs/10/).[14]

But this isn't a story about software. Since they first appeared, content management systems have looked to many companies like a way to buy and automate editorial processes that actually require a lot of time from skilled, paid human beings. People who manage content do routinely use content management systems, but they also frequently:

- Develop CMS requirements
- Define information workflows
- Deal with version control
- Manage the preservation of information (archiving and backup)
- Implement and optimize site-search tools and processes
- Define and maintain taxonomies, tagging systems, and metadata

Most content management on the web happens under the guise of another role. Some people who do content management are web editors. Others are information architects, user experience generalists, webmasters, community moderators, or all-around IT staff members. On the other hand, there's also an entire professional field—digital curation—complete with academic and professional journals, curricula, and PhD programs, that deals exclusively with the preservation and retrieval of content.

Cross-training

In addition to being descended from other fields, content work can never be fully extricated from the sibling disciplines that surround it. Content strategists need to understand enough about visual design to know when content is being presented in a way that is attractive and easy to read; they need to know enough about accessibility to plan for making content available on a wide range of devices and to users with disabilities and special access requirements; they need to know enough about search engines to make content discoverable to users of internal and external search tools, and to hold their own in conversations with SEO-maddened marketing managers.

Finally, there is the question of content development. In its purest form, content strategy does not produce content. It produces plans, guidelines, schedules, and goals for content, but not the substance itself, except inasmuch as examples are required to illustrate strategic recommendations. But if you have the ability to create good content, you'll have a real advantage over content strategists who do not.

And now, enough of theory. It's time to take a closer look at the ways in which all these abstractions play out in the real world.

---

1. The long URL: http://en.wikipedia.org/wiki/Take_point
2. Kristina Halvorson, *Content Strategy for the Web*, (California: New Riders, 2009), 75.
3. Arthur Plotnik, *The Elements of Editing*, (New York: Collier Books, 1982), 25.
4. The long URL: http://predicate-llc.com/media/presentation/the-day-2-problem-a-tour-of-editorial-strategy/
5. The long URL (subscription required): http://www.oed.com/viewdictionaryentry/Entry/45960
6. The long URL: http://www.artlies.org/article.php?id=1655&issue=59&s=1
7. The long URL: http://blog.braintraffic.com/2010/06/curation-nation/#comment-57973136
8. Hans Ulrich Obrist, *A Brief History of Curating*, (Zürich: JRP|Ringier & Les Presses du Réel, 2009), 179.
9. John Walsh's essay, "Pictures, Tears, Lights, and Seats" includes an astute analysis of presentness as it relates to curation. John B. Cuno, *Whose Muse: Art Museums and the Public Trust*, (Princeton: Princeton University Press, 2004), 84.
10. Obrist, *A Brief History of Curating*, 173.
11. The long URL: http://www.alistapart.com/articles/indefenseofreaders/
12. The long URL: http://www.leenjones.com/2009/02/rhetoric-mix/
13. The long URL: http://www.webanalyticsdemystified.com/content/
14. The long URL: http://wpcandy.com/presents/a-look-at-wordpress-market-share-numbers

3
TOOLS AND TECHNIQUES

THE DAY-TO-DAY WORK OF CONTENT STRATEGY confuses people for a reason. The things we do change from project to project and run the gamut from the purely analytical to the highly creative. In an industry in which the efforts of visual designers, information architects, front-end developers, and content creators can be seen center-stage when a new website launches, content strategy is a fundamentally backstage discipline.

You can't see it or click it. It's unusual for a website visitor to be able to point to a feature and say "that's the result of smart content strategy!"

Perhaps because of this opacity, I'm tempted to define the practice of content strategy primarily in terms of what it produces. But although lists of deliverables and methods can be useful, they're not enough on their own to explain how the practice works in real life.

Throughout this section, I will introduce a series of tools and techniques that I and others have used on content strategy projects, but I will also try to dig deeper and talk about the practical reasons for doing things in a particular way, and about the invisible aspects of the work that don't show up in deliverables.

All of which is a roundabout way of talking about methodologies. (Insert *Jaws* theme here.) So let's discuss them for a moment.

Methodologies

Because our discipline is new, and because we often work with user experience and web development teams with their own methodologies, the last few years have produced a host of discussions about the best way to do content strategy. Content strategy is sufficiently diverse that nearly all content workers must specialize to some extent, and our methodologies tend to reflect that specialization.

- A content strategist primarily concerned with **marketing communication** usually focuses on branding and messages, effective cross-channel outreach, the creation of persuasive content, and the development of sustainable publishing processes. Her methodology will need to support these activities.
- On the other hand, a content strategist who focuses on **information management** will need a methodology that accommodates technical analysis, data modeling, and large-scale content reuse across multiple systems (websites, intranets, customer relationship management systems, etc.).
- Content specialists who work alongside **user experience consultants** or as a part of **web development teams** may need a methodology that works with marketing, educational, and technical content, and that accommodates on-site and off-site search, content taxonomies, CMS requirements development, and information architecture.

Whatever your situation or degree of specialization, you will need a methodology that supports the work you actually perform—and you'll probably need to refine it from time to time to make sure it's still appropriate. My own methodology is simple, and has emerged from my background as an online editorial strategist who usually works with user experience and web development teams. Although the deliverables and individual processes I use vary from project to project, all my work falls into three categories:

- **Evaluate**
- **Design**
- **Execute**

This isn't a chronology for each project—though each project will include all three phases—but a repeatable sequence to be followed in ways big and small throughout time-bounded projects and in the long-term maintenance of content.

- **Evaluation** happens at the beginning of a project, and then again at the very end—and sometimes at the end of each phase. Research of all kinds falls under evaluation, as do usability testing and traffic analysis.
- **Design** here doesn't mean visual design. It includes high-level communication strategy and proposals for public-facing and back-end features related to content. It also includes the design of tactical plans for creating and revising content and the design of tools and processes for long-term management of content.
- **Execution** refers to all the things we do to turn strategies into reality: writing and revising content, setting up publishing workflows, sourcing and aggregating content, and so on. Even on projects on which I'm not directly responsible for execution, I still create examples to illustrate recommendations, and this too is a form of execution.

Though you should feel free to use it, I don't offer my own methodology as the One True Way, but as an example of a methodology optimized for performing certain kinds of content work.

And now, let's take a look at the work itself.

THE THINGS WE MAKE

Before we dive in, a note about "deliverables"—those things we give or "deliver" to clients. It's a ridiculous, clumsy word. Unfortunately, the circumlocutions required to get around it are awful, too, so I'm going to keep using it. And hey, it could be worse—at least our industry mostly avoids "work product."

Here's a completely non-comprehensive list of deliverables you might use while doing content strategy:

- Accessibility guidelines
- Benchmarks
- Channel strategy
- CMS requirements
- Communication plans
- Community and social strategy
- Community moderation policies
- Competitive analyses
- Content production workshops
- Content sourcing plans
- Content style guides
- Content templates
- Editorial calendars
- Example content
- Feature descriptions
- Gap analyses
- Metadata recommendations
- Project proposals
- Publishing workflow
- Qualitative content audit and findings
- Quantitative content audit and findings
- Resource review (people, tools, time)
- Search-engine optimization reviews
- Success metrics
- Taxonomies
- Traffic analysis
- Usability tests

- User personas
- User research findings
- User research plans
- User scenarios
- Visual presentation recommendations
- Wireframes
- Workflow recommendations

With one exception, I will offer overviews of documents and processes, rather than detailed instructions. You can find references for many of these documents at http://incisive.nu/elements. One lovely thing about being such a chatty discipline is that someone, somewhere is probably writing a blog post right this minute about whatever you might want to know.

The content strategist's children go...shoeless?

Content strategy incorporates a wider range of processes and deliverables than do most of its sibling fields, and one thing we rarely discuss is how to choose the best approach for each project. As a result, we often stick to the same few easily repeated techniques, even when they're not the ones best suited to a particular project. When we do that, we miss the chance to do better and more interesting work.

Every deliverable you create and every meeting you lead deals with two kinds of strategy: the one you're developing for the project, and the one you're using to guide your own communication with your colleagues, employers, and clients. These people usually won't be your target audience for the *project*, but they are the audience for your *deliverables*. I'm not suggesting that we do full-scale user research and strategy for each client or document—if we did, we'd never get anything else done—but we can think strategically about our work.

By phase: when does it happen?

The most obvious way of grouping deliverables is by project phase, especially if you're a consultant. You may have your own terms for each phase, but whether you work with an agency or alone, you're probably familiar with a process that looks something like this (FIG 2):

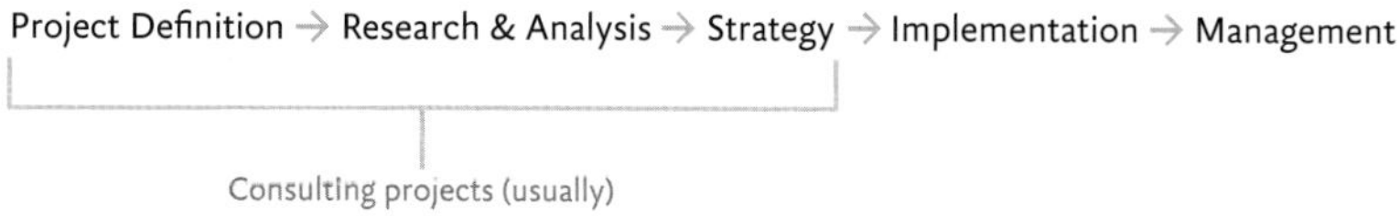

Project Definition → Research & Analysis → Strategy → Implementation → Management

Consulting projects (usually)

FIG 2: A progression of phases within user experience and content strategy projects.

If you're working with a design team, breaking down your work by project phase can help your colleagues in other disciplines understand how your work will interact with theirs. It can also help clients understand how your work fits into the project as a whole.

The problem with this method of thinking and talking about content strategy is that it doesn't say much about what the work really looks like. If your teammates or clients aren't familiar with content strategy, you'll need to say more about your work than how it fits into the project timeline. One good place to begin is with the function or purpose of your content strategy deliverables.

By function: what does it do?

A second way to look at our work is to consider what each tool or process is meant to accomplish. Think of this as a detailed, project-specific version of developing a methodology. On a very high level, you need to know what you intend to accomplish, either with a content strategy project or over the long term in a content strategy role. Once you understand the highest-level goal, you can work backward to figure out what you need to produce.

Here's an example. Say I'm working alongside a user experience team to redesign a website for a large consultancy. The company's website contains more than 5,000 pieces of content, and its publishing system is distributed across a dozen divisions and locations. The project brief explains that our top three goals are to align the company's online presence with its brand, to make it easier for potential customers to find the information they need, and to bring consistency to the website sections managed by its various divisions.

Going back to my underlying methodology, I can work out what I need to do to accomplish our goals:

- **Evaluate**: Quantitative and qualitative content audit; traffic analysis; competitive review; user research, personas, and scenarios (in collaboration with user experience); publishing process analysis.

- **Design**: Communication brief (explains project goals in detail); high-level and detailed recommendations on overall messages, what kind of content to add, what to get rid of, and how to communicate with the site's various audiences; metadata recommendations (in collaboration with technology team members); editorial style guidelines; publishing workflow; content sourcing and aggregation plan; cross-channel communication recommendations; success metrics and analysis plan.

- **Execute**: Example content for each major content type; content templates to support the development of new content pre- and post-launch; content creation and publishing workshop; editorial style guide.

That's it. Thinking about function can help shake content work loose from the clichés and habits of paint-by-numbers delivery, and it helps to know what you're trying to accomplish with each deliverable and process before you dive in and start trying to do it.

By method: how does it work?

You might also consider placing each deliverable you develop on a continuum with objective, analytical work at one end and subjective, creative work at the other. This approach can be particularly helpful when you work with clients or colleagues who haven't ever seen a content strategy document and don't know whether to expect naked spreadsheets or prosy conceptual recommendations.

If I plot some of the deliverables I work with most frequently on a chart according to their function (I'll just use evaluate vs. design for this example) and their nature (analytical vs. creative), it looks something like this (FIG 3):

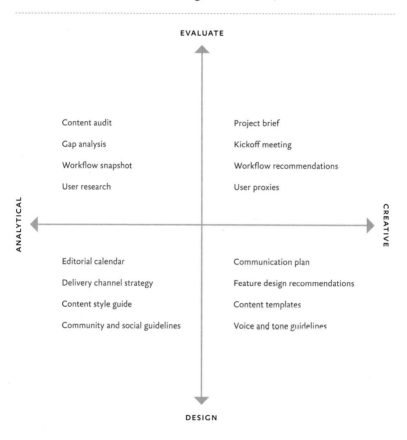

FIG 3: Content deliverables and processes plotted according to function and nature.

In real life, few content documents are 100% analytical, and almost none are 100% creative, but having a sense of the character of each piece of work can help streamline the development process. If you're working with a team of content people, this sort of breakdown can also help you figure out how to divide up the work in a way that takes advantage of your colleagues' various skills. Got a data nerd handy? Put her on that content audit and gap analysis. And your content specialist who used to edit a magazine? Let him lead the feature design recommendations and voice and tone work.

By audience: who is it for?

Programmers rarely present raw code in client meetings. For every visual design comp or interface prototype that goes to the client (or manager), there are dozens or hundreds of cocktail-napkin and whiteboard sketches that no one outside the core team ever sees. In the same way, we should resist the temptation to show our clients everything we make.

Some documents are for you alone, to refine your thinking and organize your work; some are best used by information architects, visual designers, or CMS developers; some are intended to offer ideas to clients for approval or revision. Each may be valuable, but it's quite rare for all of them to have the same audience. Some clients are not best served by spreadsheets or detailed content docs—they need executive summaries and any pertinent questions that have arisen during the document's development, but not the thing itself. Conversely, members of our own teams often require details that clients and managers don't. Information architects, for example, often need to know far more about the nature, structure, and relative importance of each kind of content than a client will ever want to see.

Give people what they need, and don't deluge them with things they don't. Some clients will want to see absolutely everything, but if you make a general rule of showing less, your approval cycles may move more quickly—and you won't have to say "That's not really something we can talk about just yet" more than three or four times per presentation.

Consider your audience in the selection, introduction, and preparation of your deliverables, and even your most over-worked client or manager will have an easier time giving you the feedback and approval you need.

On being an advocate

Nearly every project contains within it two sets of needs that are held in tension: the needs of the client and the needs of the user. In successful projects, these two sets of needs tend to be complementary, but you will also encounter situations in which client and user needs appear to conflict. In this situation, content specialists are well placed to act as user advocates, as we often have an easier time finding and citing user research to back up our positions than do visual designers held hostage by a client's personal fondness for mauve.

In practice, this means that when someone dictates that a certain piece of content must be on the homepage (or landing page, or moral equivalent) you should try to discover whether doing so helps users. If it doesn't, you may not be able to discard the directive entirely; these instructions often emerge from intractable internal political conflicts. But if you can suss out the reasoning behind the request, you may be able to suggest alterations that make the content more useful, or recommend a prominent alternative placement that would benefit more readers.

This can be every bit as interpersonally fiddly as it sounds, but it's a learnable skill. A few things to keep in mind:

- Acting as a user advocate doesn't make you an impractical idealist. As we've learned from our editorial colleagues, if your content doesn't work for the user, you've already failed. User advocacy is simply a way of ensuring that a project achieves business goals.
- The personas or other user proxies that you or your colleagues have created are the best backup you could hope for. Return to these tools when you need to validate opinions—yours or someone else's.

- It's very easy for content specialists to be drawn into internal conflicts. Don't let it happen.

Content strategists must also act as advocates for content, which is a slightly different proposition. Whenever someone proposes a new feature or a major change in plan, you need to (tactfully) discover the content requirements that accompany that decision and determine whether or not they're realistic.

PROJECT DEFINITION

Whether you're working as a consultant or doing an in-house project, anything bigger than routine publishing and maintenance needs a project definition phase. On very large projects, such a phase might take months. For a small in-house revamp project, it might take fifteen minutes. What matters is that you take the time to clarify what the project is meant to accomplish—and to make sure that everyone who needs to agree on that point, does.

What are we doing and why?

For consultants, project definition usually begins with an RFP ("request for proposal") or other initiating document from the client. Content work can't be divorced from business goals, so content people need to know as much as possible about the client's understanding of their goals. If you're coming in after the contract has been signed, always ask to see these documents and any proposals created in response to them, and make sure content strategy is represented at internal and client kick-off meetings.

Complex projects usually require the preparation of a *creative brief* or *communication brief* or *project summary*: a document that clearly explains what your team is expected to do. If you want the project to go smoothly, make sure you contribute to this document so that content needs are integrated from the beginning.

If you're on an internal team, you probably won't see anything as formal as an RFP and proposal, but don't neglect project definition. Internal projects are notoriously difficult to pin down, and if the goals and requirements of your decision-makers are allowed to remain nebulous, the project will suffer later on.

Meet the stakeholders

Whether you're a consultant or on staff, you'll want to conduct (or observe) stakeholder research.

Stakeholders are the people on the client side who are responsible for or strongly interested in a project's success. On a large project, stakeholders will probably include executives, department or team leaders, and the internal staff members who work most closely with content or with the website on the whole. On a small project, you may need to conduct only a handful of stakeholder interviews; on a very large project for a big organization, you may need several dozen.

Planning stakeholder interviews—and becoming a good interviewer in general—requires thought and experience. It's a skill worth learning, even if you plan to piggyback your work on research conducted by others, because no matter how good your initial interview plan is, you'll almost certainly need to ask follow-up questions once the project is underway.

Once you've scooped up all the information you can from RFPs, proposals, kickoff meetings, and stakeholder interviews, it's time to distill it into something you can use. In Chapter 5 of *Content Strategy for the Web,* Kristina Halvorson offers an exceptionally sane and practical method of organizing this sort of information, based on processes developed in collaboration with Brain Traffic's Melissa Rach. This method divides the information you receive from clients or managers into *business goals, tactics, requirements,* and *project objectives,* with big circles and stars drawn around the project objectives. To paraphrase Kristina:

- Business goals are the overarching aims that an entire organization tries to achieve. To select a well-known example, one of Google's business goals is "Don't be evil."

- Tactics are all the detailed, specific requests you'll hear again and again in stakeholder interviews. "Clarify navigation" and "improve search" are two that come up a lot.
- Requirements are the project's immovable objects: launch date, project budget, available staff members, and so on.
- Project objectives live under business goals and above tactics, while respecting requirements. They are things you can actually accomplish with content strategy, like "change our website to reflect our new organizational focus on education."

Seriously, this section is worth the purchase price of the book all on its own, so go buy it and read it.

How do I know when it's love?

To complete the project definition phase, you'll need to know what "success" means for the project—and that means you have to decide what to measure. Some people call this stuff "success metrics," which is pretty clear, but I like "victory conditions," a term borrowed from the game design world. In chess, the victory condition is checkmate. In War, it's not running out of cards. In the game of Go, it's controlling the most territory. In all these cases, it's clear what you have to do to win, and that's a great quality to emulate.

A measure of success that cannot, in fact, be measured is a lousy measure of success. Try to turn as many soft, aspirational goals as possible into success criteria, and make them specific enough that you can actually tell whether or not you've met them. If you're trying to increase traffic or sign-ups, what numbers will you try to hit? Are those numbers possible and realistic? When do you need to reach them for it to count as a victory? How will you tell if you've achieved other, softer goals?

After you've documented victory conditions for your project, it's a good idea to collect all your project definition information in one place. If you show it to your client or employer, you may even want to create a formal summary in the form of a *project brief* or *communication brief*.

RESEARCH & ASSESSMENT

Now that you know all about your project goals and your clients' desires, it's time to begin the real research.

Users: who they are and what they want

Modern web development teams usually begin projects by conducting user research and developing tools that keep user needs at the project's center; the same is true for content-only engagements. The purpose of user research is to move beyond assumptions, guesses, and stereotypes to discover what your human readers, viewers, and listeners really want and need.

Who conducts user research? It depends on the project. Information architects and user experience designers have pioneered most of the techniques involved and frequently do the research themselves, but content strategists can make perfectly good researchers. My own preference is to work with an IA or UX person whenever possible, including the user research phase.

Internal teams are often tempted to rely on their gradually accrued and informal understanding of their users. This kind of knowledge is valuable, but if you don't supplement it with disciplined research, you risk missing important but submerged needs. If you're working on an informal internal project, you may be tempted to put off user research until you've developed a "first pass" at content. Just remind yourself that even if you meet all project requirements and fully understand what your employers expect to see, if people don't read, watch, or listen to your content, you've failed.

Interviews, then proxies

Interviews are usually the first step, and as with stakeholder interviews, there is an art to selecting and interviewing participants. The finesse with which you approach this work can dramatically affect the usefulness of the information you receive.

Once you or your team have completed your initial user interviews, you can develop *user proxies*. These stand-ins for individual users synthesize the information you've learned and give your team a set of likely user needs and actions they can use to validate their ideas. User proxies include *personas, user scenarios, use cases,* and *activity flows,* all of which have been discussed extensively elsewhere. In the end, it matters less whether you create fancy, formal documents or draw stick figures on a whiteboard. What matters is that someone gets it done.

Around the time you're conducting user research, you can begin a review of the project's existing content. Doing these two quite different kinds of research at the same time may feel a bit daunting, but it's a great way to make sure that you're thoroughly immersed in your client's world—and that of their users.

Welcome to the spreadsheet: content inventories

Before we go much further, we need to discover what content already exists; this step is often called a quantitative audit or content inventory. The web is full of useful advice on conducting content audits, so I'll stick to a brief summary. Essentially, you're going to create an extremely detailed site map that represents every page and other piece of content on the website you are working with, along with every other piece of existing content that may end up on the site, but that currently lives elsewhere.

For each piece of content, an inventory generally lists a:

- title,
- format (standard text, video, PDF, etc.),
- URL or other location,
- content type (landing page, article, support page, contact page, etc.), and
- "owner" (person responsible for upkeep).

In my office, big inventories involve a lot of black coffee, a few late nights, and a playlist of questionable but cheering music prominently featuring the soundtrack of object-collection video game Katamari Damacy. It takes quite awhile to exhaustively inventory a large site, but it's the only way to really understand what you have to work with.

Culling the herd: qualitative audits

At some point during or after your inventory, you'll want to conduct a qualitative audit of some or all of your existing content. As you've doubtless gathered, that involves assessing the quality of the content. This may sound straightforward, but there is one major challenge: how do you evaluate content when you don't know what you're looking for? Sure, you can tell if content is badly written, but until you know more about your users' needs, how will you know if the content is working?

You can't. And that's the main thing that affects the timing of a qualitative audit. Unless the audit timing is entirely out of your control, plan to have your user research complete and a few personas or other proxies on hand before you begin evaluating quality. Doing so will allow you to assess your content based on the basic principles outlined in the first section of this book: Is it appropriate? Useful and user-centered? Clear, consistent, and concise? Has it been properly supported, or is it outdated or inaccurate?

How you measure those qualities is up to you, and you'll also have to decide whether or not you have the time and resources to complete a full audit of all the content you've inventoried, or if you need to focus on representative sections alone.

Later on, when you begin recommending changes, you'll need to be able to tell your client or manager how much work it will take to implement your recommendations. Audits are how you find that out. (If you're working internally or doing maintenance, they're also a brilliant foundation for ongoing quality checks and content updates.)

Other resources

There's more to resource assessment than content audits. For medium-sized and large projects, you'll want to document the publishing workflow: how content is planned, created, approved, produced, and maintained. You'll also need to know who is available to create and revise content in the short term, and what content budgets look like so you can make realistic recommendations about content development and upkeep.

If you're designing a site from scratch, you won't have much content to audit, but you should still document available content resources: writers, illustrators or other content producers, photograph collections, existing multimedia, production resources like studio time, and so on.

Finally, this is the time to:

- conduct any search-engine and traffic analysis indicated during project definition,
- do any usability or accessibility reviews appropriate to the project, and
- document the current state of applicable internationalization, localization, and translation initiatives.

You may find that you're able to integrate some or all of these processes into the content inventory and audit. Once you're done with everything, write up a short summary describing your process, criteria for evaluation, and major findings. This findings document will be useful to a much larger audience than your spreadsheets.

How green *is* their grass?

A *competitive review* generally means a mini-audit of content published by organizations that compete with yours (or your client's)—although for some projects, a competitive review may not actually be about competitors. For a project with one company division, you might review the content practices of other divisions as well as those of external rivals. For nonprofit organizations, you may be better off reviewing sites that accomplish parallel tasks, or organizations with similar audiences or brands, than trying to study only organizations that work in the same sector as yours.

Instead of filling spreadsheets with detailed content reviews, you can almost always get away with a lighter touch during a competitive review. Go through the content you've identified for review in a systematic way, describing in general terms what you find, making special note of any features or content that stand out as particularly excellent or especially awful. In the end, you should have a general sense of "what's out there" as well as a list of things that seem to work well and things that are definitely to be avoided.

Synthesis

Once you've collected all this information, it's time to figure out what you've really learned. You might take this opportunity to produce a formal, twenty-page report, or you might simply send a few emails and have some conversations in the hallway; the ideal is probably somewhere in between.

This is a good time to convey the highlights of your content audits and competitive reviews, including any "quick fix" remedies (fix broken pages, correct misspellings and inaccurate facts, switch inaccessible files to accessible versions) that can be applied to the current site without slowing the rest of the project down. It's also a good time to amend the project brief to document anything you've learned that has changed your fundamental understanding of the project.

In the end, what matters is that your colleagues understand the research results in ways that will let them do better work, and that your client understands the implications of the results for the remainder of the project.

STRATEGY AND DESIGN

Once you have defined clear project goals and measures of success, and achieved a thorough understanding of user needs and existing resources, you're ready to begin the strategy part of content strategy. This means taking everything you've learned in the first two phases of the project and developing a set of concepts, plans, and guidelines for creating and maintaining content that meets user needs and project goals.

As you read the pages that follow, you may wonder why all of these content recommendations and guidelines aren't simply created and delivered all at once. On small or informal projects, some of them can be, and even on larger projects, you can usually present several kinds of work to the client at the same time. I've presented them in the sequence you see here because especially on larger projects, each batch of work feeds the next. Without understanding your core messages and the structure of your site, you can't make recommendations on communicating those messages *within* the site structure; without approval for major changes and big new ideas, it's folly to flesh out the tiny but important details that will bring those concepts to life.

Like visual design and information architecture, content strategy is an iterative process, moving gradually from the general to the specific. Back in the 1990s, when you loaded a webpage with inline JPEG images, they started out looking like classic Nintendo characters and gradually came into focus. So too will your content strategy work gradually evolve from blocky, abstract outlines into crisp photographic detail.

Messages

Some projects and organizations require content strategy work that focuses primarily on streamlining existing content, filling a few gaps here and there, and establishing solid, sustainable processes for workflow and governance. Others require substantial creative development work and the advancement of new concepts.

Either way, you need to document the main ideas—the messages discussed in Chapter 1—which you will convey to your users. Each separate audience will probably have its own subset of messages that lives under the umbrella of site-wide messages. If the organization already has a list of messages to be communicated, you can simply adopt those that make sense for your project. If they don't, you'll need to collaborate with the appropriate teams to develop one. Don't be afraid to give homework to the client, or to your marketing/corporate communications people, if you're on staff.

Although you may develop some messages from whole cloth, most will probably emerge from your client's existing communication strategy. If you lack a communication strategy on which to build your content work, plan to spend extra time getting approval for your high-level recommendations, because they're likely to spark substantial internal debate. Don't get bogged down on message development. Messages are important, but they're an internal tool, and as such, should be developed only to the point of optimum usefulness. Spending an extra week fiddling with message copy means losing a week you probably can't afford to lose. As Halvorson notes:[1]

Messages aren't content. They're used to shape content. So, as you create your content for each page and component, you'll interpret the messaging for the audience and page context.

Once you have the main ideas you need to communicate arranged in a hierarchy, validate them with the client, revise, and move on.

Big concepts

As you begin to understand the structure of your content, you may wish to begin introducing major departures from the existing content and features to your colleagues and client. Not at the wireframe level, or by talking about specific pages— it's not time for that yet. Think of this part of the project as the equivalent of a particularly sexy pitch in the advertising world: you're introducing new concepts and big ideas, not tweaks and minor revisions.

There are two reasons to introduce major conceptual changes before structural design begins. First, by explicitly introducing big changes as *strategies*, you'll be able to discover gaps in your assumptions and make any required course corrections before you begin developing tactical plans. Second, when you introduce new concepts early on, you give large, complex organizations a chance to ease into new ways of thinking. Doing so almost always softens reflexive resistance to new ideas and gives you (and your champions on the client team) time to allay fears and win over dubious stakeholders. So what qualifies as a major concept?

- Substantial shifts in target audience
- Important new content-related features—blogs, podcasts, wikis and other knowledge bases, editorial features (articles, essays, case studies), video tutorials, and so on
- Big changes in voice and tone

Conceptual recommendations should always include the strategic rationale behind the proposed change, and should support this rationale with findings from user, stakeholder, and competitive research.

Once you have approval for the general ideas and concepts that will shape content for your project, you can begin to assemble plans and recommendations for actual content. You may wish to create a detailed set of guidelines and content needs for each site section and delivery channel, or you may only need brief written guidelines combined with content templates and examples of good and bad content.

Structural design

At some point in every online project, someone has to decide what's going to be on a website, and sometimes what's going to be included on other channels as well. This sequence of decisions will take into account all the work done in the project definition phase and everything discovered through user research and competitive reviews to create a structural design that meets user needs and serves business goals. The results may include a *sitemap* and a set of *wireframes* (replaced on some projects by *page description diagrams*), sometimes accompanied by *user flows*.

So is this an information architecture thing, or a part of content strategy?

This is a great question, and there are lots of answers—no two alike: *Information architecture is a subset of content strategy. Content strategy functions should be folded into information architecture like blueberries into muffin batter. User experience design includes everything, content or otherwise.*

In my experience, it is very easy for brilliant information architects (or UX people who do information architecture) to underestimate the importance of editorial planning, voice and tone, and detailed guidelines for content creation. And conversely, it's very easy for highly skilled content people to underestimate how much information architecture has to do with things other than content: the finicky details of application behavior and interaction design, in particular. I'm a huge fan of collaborations between information architects who care about editorial concerns and content strategists who love structure and talking about data. But whatever your situation, it's important to know your way around structural design, if only so that you can provide useful feedback and support.

That said, you won't find Information Architecture 101 in this text. In the last twenty years, information architecture—and its interaction design and user experience design cousins—have developed into highly sophisticated fields with substantial bodies of professional literature. Even if you only dip your toe into the waters of structural design, I recommend that you take the time to learn the basics of IA design principles, methodologies, and deliverables.

Site-level content recommendations

Once you have a sitemap and wireframes to work with you'll be able to return to the business goals and user needs you collected at the beginning of the project and begin fleshing out the details of your content plan.

Large websites with lots of content will benefit from content recommendations for each section of the site as depicted in the site map and wireframes. This is primarily an organizational exercise, as you will have collected the pertinent information in previous phases.

Think of this as your last chance to talk about underlying strategies, because it's all tactical planning from here on out. High-level content recommendations typically include some or all of the following:

- Primary and secondary messages to be communicated in each section's content
- Primary (and sometimes secondary) audiences to be served by each section's content
- Notes on the integration of major new content-related features into the site
- Early recommendations on voice and tone
- Recommendations on integrating community features (comments, forums, etc.)
- A discussion of how each of the site's major audiences will be served by its content
- Recommendations on delivery channels for the various kinds of content you're working with (website vs. email vs. social networks, etc.)

Page-level content guidelines

Wireframes are wonderful things. They allow information architects to represent structure without implying anything about visual design, and they give content strategists a skeleton outline on which to arrange content. But although they often look like they're representing the function of each page, they necessarily leave out a lot of detail that will be critically important to the people who eventually develop the site's content—like what the content on each page is supposed to accomplish, how it relates to content elsewhere on the site, where the content will come from, and how it's supposed to look and sound.

Unless you're working on a very small project, you'll want to develop content guidelines to go alongside the wireframes. I use a combination of detailed written recommendations, a content style guide, and content templates (described below) to communicate these guidelines. Depending on the project's scope and goals—as documented in the project definition phase—the written guidelines will include some or all of the following:

- Site-wide and section-specific voice and tone guidelines
- Strategies for cross-linking content throughout the site
- Notes on the integration of advertising content, when applicable
- Social and community guidelines and policies
- Recommendations on creating useful and accessible multimedia content
- Plans for metadata (data that describes other data)

A content style guide includes notes on the choice of a standard style guide, house style guidelines (deviations from or additions to the standard style guide), specifications for images and multimedia, and guidelines for non-standard style in social media or other channels (executive blogs, for example).

The contents of the written recommendations and style guide will be reinforced in an even more detailed deliverable called a content template.

Content templates in 60 seconds

A content template is a simple document that serves two purposes: it's a paragraph-level companion to your website's wireframes, and it's a simple, effective means of getting useful information from the people who have information to the people who can communicate that information. Each template contains information about a specific kind of page (or content module) on your website: section landing pages, articles, product pages, staff bios, job listings, and so on.

By providing your experts with a fill-in-the-blank structure for their content drafts, you can be quite explicit about what you do (and don't) want—and can help save your writers from the hypnotic blink of a cursor on a blank page, to which so many have fallen victim.

Of course, before you can create content templates, you need to decide what each page is intended to do. The purpose of each page should emerge from a combination of your user and stakeholder research, the messages you've documented, and the wireframes you're working with. You'll also need to have a pretty good idea of how the new structure represented in the sitemap and wireframes matches up to content that already exists—for this, you'll need to return to the content inventory and look for matches between new content needs and old content resources.

After that, you can make a content template in four easy steps (FIG 4):

1. In a text document, list each piece of information that must be on the page, followed by optional pieces of information.
2. After the name of each chunk of content, note what that content is supposed to accomplish. For example, if article abstracts appear in public search results as well as internal content management tools, they need to be intelligible to external audiences. A list of product benefits should focus on how the product will help your target readers.
3. List your specifications for each piece of content: ideal word count, capitalization style, list vs. paragraph vs. heading, and any notes like "avoid jargon in this section—look for words that will make sense to a non-specialist" or "if you can replace this description with a screenshot and a good caption, do it."
4. Provide example content for each piece of content on the template. For pieces that can be created in several ways (a list or a paragraph, a screenshot or video clip), provide examples of all options whenever possible.

PLANNING FOR CONTENT CREATION

Content creation encompasses writing, illustration, information visualization, metadata and text-equivalent production, and interface writing, and is supported by creative direction and old-fashioned editorial leadership.

You may notice that I have not written "web writing," and there's a reason for that: While it's true that writing for the web is different from writing for print, it is also increasingly true that "the web" is only one part of a larger internet publishing landscape. We do write for the web, but we also write for applications, email, mobile, and a horde of services that straddle multiple categories.

This is not a writing manual, nor a book about communication in general—not because these aren't vital, central tasks, but because the world doesn't need another book about web writing basics and the principles of visual communication. But all content strategists need to understand the challenges inherent in content development, and to be able to direct the production of content that meets the project's requirements.

There are only three ways to produce content. You can get it from dedicated creators, from internal experts, or you can avoid the issue entirely by aggregating someone else's content. In the fantasy world from which many marketing plans spring, these three methods are equally useful and entirely distinct. In reality, they are complex, messy, and often inseparable from each other.

Dedicated creators

- **Pros**: Dedicated freelance or staff writers/video producers/communicators will have the time required to create the content you need. They'll also be really good at their jobs (or you wouldn't have hired them).
- **Cons**: No matter who will write your text or create your illustrations and videos, someone must decide what they will communicate. If your content needs to sell the benefits of a complex product or educate readers about a complicated process, it's unrealistic to expect that a freelance writer or web editor will be able to write knowledgeably about the subject without access to internal experts.

CONTENT TEMPLATE

Section Name: Page Title

Audit Identifier: 2.1.4   **URL:** http://www.widgetcorp.com

Audiences:	Decision-makers within small manufacturing firms (primary), engineers (secondary)
Primary message:	Insert here the primary message to be communicated throughout the project.
Audience-specific messages:	Include messages designed specifically for the audiences above, or associated with specific site sections or product lines.
Purpose of page:	Generate sales by communicating product benefits to decision-makers in small manufacturing firms.
Style and tone notes:	Straightforward style, using short sentences and clear, strong verbs. This page serves a limited and specialized audience, so if you occasionally need to use technical jargon to communicate clearly and efficiently, go ahead. Prefer "you" to "I" and "we" constructions.

Product Description ("What is it?")

Product Name: Ultra Deluxe Widget   **Name of Product Line:** Superwidget Suite 2011

Short product description (2-3 sentences):

The description should include at least one noun that describes the product— besides its name.

Type description here. This is essentially the product's elevator pitch in two or three short sentences. It should answer the questions "What is it?" "Who is it for?" and "What does it do?"

Example product description:

Widget Corp's Ultra Deluxe Widget is an inverse reactive current supply mechanism used for operating nofer-trunnions and reducing sinusoidal depleneration when used in conjunction with a drawn reciprocating dingle arm.

(This is where you would provide real or plausible example copy for each chunk of content. Ideally, you'll have 2-3 examples for each major chunk of content.)

FIG 4: A sample content template for WidgetCorp's product pages. Product vocabulary borrowed from http://bkaprt.com/cs/11/.[2]

For product packages with variable discounts, enter telephone and email info for the relevant sales team.

Benefits are customer-focused and answer the question, "What will this product do for me?"

Features are about the product and answer the question, "How will the product accomplish this benefit?"

Be as specific as you can with benefits. How much can costs be reduced? What increases in efficiency can customers expect?

Sales contact information: Link to purchase page or contact numbers/emails.

Product Benefits & Features ("How will it help me?")

Benefit/feature pairs:

- Benefit/feature pair #1. Lead with the benefit and then follow with the feature or features that make it possible.
- Benefit/feature pair #2
- Benefit/feature pair #3

Examples:

- *Cuts maintenance costs in half by replacing delicate gremlin studs with a robust spiral decommutator and eliminates the need for drammock oil.*
- *Prevents side fumbling via the addition of pentametric fan consisting of six hydrocoptic marzelvanes fitted to the ambifacient lunar vaneshaft.*
- *Increases production capacity by up to 15% through the use of a streamlined regurgitative purwell nubbled with a superaminative wennel-sprocket.*

Optional Info: ("What's included?" "How does it work?")

Depending on the product, you may want to include some of the following optional details:

- **Features List**—Some products have more important features than can be easily worked into a short benefits list. Those features would go here. This element does not replace the benefits list that goes on the first page.
- **Feature Table**—Compares a single Widget Corp product to similar products produced by competitors, or compares various widget configurations within a Widget Corp product line.
- **New!**—A paragraph or bulleted list briefly detailing new features after an update to the product line.

Internal experts

- **Pros**: If you get people already on staff to create content, they will almost certainly have the right subject-matter knowledge. They'll also often know the target audience inside and out, especially if they have a marketing background. Plus, they'll know the existing company culture—which can be either a benefit or a danger.
- **Cons**: The people with topical expertise are often too busy to produce content or unable to communicate their expertise in a way that serves the intended audience. One of the great challenges of content strategy—and especially of content production—is getting ideas from the heads of experts into the heads of content producers. If you rely on internal experts without a dedicated editor and approval process, you're courting trouble.

Content curation

You might attempt to avoid the complexities of working with outside writers or internal experts by "curating"—or aggregating—content created by and for someone else.

- **Pros**: By linking to a carefully chosen selection of content from elsewhere on the internet, and by annotating and framing this content in ways that add to the discussion, you can serve readers who don't have the time to find the content on their own, or who rely on your editorial viewpoints.
- **Cons**: May be seen as a quick, cheap alternative to creating original content—after all, how hard can it be to just collect links to other people's work? But large-scale content curation is neither simple nor inexpensive. Done well, it requires the time and attention of someone who has a nose for interesting information, and who has the editorial ability to assemble compelling narratives from the material they collect.

Worst of all, because it's a popular trend, content curation may be selected for the wrong reasons—because it's a buzzword and a seemingly simple way to pump out large quantities of content, rather than because it meets demonstrated user needs. And since resources are finite, tactics that don't serve user needs divert resources from tactics that do. Like blogging, content curation can be a useful component of a larger content plan, but over time, it requires substantial quantities of time and attention.

Getting it done

So! To summarize, content development is tricky and takes time and money. But there are plenty of things you can do to make it easier and more efficient.

- Designate an editorial lead with strong organizational and editorial skills. Whether you rely on internal writers or hire outside creators, this person will manage the content development process. Give that person as much authority and backup as possible. If the leaders of your organization make it clear to internal writers that your content lead's requests are high priority, the work tends to magically get itself done.
- If you have dedicated content producers, help them set up in-person, telephone, or email interviews for collecting the information needed to write the content. Plan on more than one round of interviews, as the first round almost always raises as many questions as it answers.
- After that, plan on a factual review of the final content by the expert in question to make sure that their information has come through intact. Experts who speak only jargon or who aren't especially good communicators can still do factual reviews, and content producers should have backup in their attempt to keep fluff and jargon out of final content.

- Before you begin asking for content (or raw information) from internal experts, persuade someone in a leadership position to communicate with them—preferably in a group, and ideally in person—about the kind of content you need, the ways in which the content will benefit the experts' departments, and the relevant deadlines. Doing so can dissolve lingering internal resistance, soothe frazzled nerves, and convey the strategic importance of the work.
- If your internal sources are genuinely overworked, seek concrete ways of temporarily reducing the experts' workload—perhaps by delaying other work or temporarily cutting a routine but non-critical process—so that they can produce the content you need.
- Create detailed descriptions of the kind of content you need to receive. Content templates can be hugely helpful.
- If the deadline is approaching and content isn't flowing despite your attempts to explain the project and free up time, consider holding a few half-day or day-long content working sessions, and require that experts who are behind their deadlines attend one or more working sessions.

PLANNING FOR CONTENT MANAGEMENT

Although some content strategy consultants assist with content maintenance, many leave projects well before long-term content management issues arise. For these consultants, it's especially important to deal with both content production and ongoing maintenance in recommendations delivered throughout the project, rather than in an afterthought that flits across the client's radar just as the project ends.

If your client has a dedicated web editor and a reasonably effective publishing process, they may not need much beyond a content style guide and advice on content reviews. But if the client's publishing process is more tenuous, you may need to help them design or overhaul their publishing and approval workflow. Editorial calendars can provide structure for ongoing content development and management, and can also encourage regular strategy discussions between content creators and the people who develop organization-wide communication strategy.

But the truth is, none of these tools can replace a skilled in-house editor. If your client will be creating and managing more than a few dozen pages of content, they'll need an editor or internal content strategist to keep things running smoothly. A staff member already involved in communications or web development may have the aptitude for this work, or the organization may need to hire an additional employee; either way, someone needs to ride herd after your consulting work is done.

The inside perspective

Those who do content strategy work from within organizations tend to fill roles quite similar to those of a traditional managing editor: they plan and oversee the communication of new themes and ideas, manage schedules, and collaborate with writers and other content producers. As importantly, they also work alongside designers, programmers, project managers, business managers, marketing teams, senior executives, human resources departments, event planners, and a horde of other stakeholders and fellow travelers to get content produced, revised, approved, and published—and to see to it that it's regularly evaluated and eventually revised or removed.

Common content management tasks include:

- Regularly scheduled editorial reviews of all content
- Ongoing traffic and findability analysis
- Community moderation and oversight, including comment-wrangling and social media interactions
- Editorial planning sessions to define changes in theme and to introduce new campaigns
- Ongoing translation and localization efforts

As more organizations realize that they must think of themselves as publishers, the world of ongoing internal editorial leadership is becoming ever more integrated into the practice of content strategy—something which can only enhance both disciplines.

A word on assessment

Within content strategy, the practice of ongoing assessment and refinement of content is just beginning to blossom. The next few years are certain to bring us dozens of new techniques and methods that will rapidly become standard practice.

We could all do much worse than to begin with the *three whole chapters about evaluation and refinement* in Colleen Jones's *Clout* (it's like Christmas, I tell you) and with the Peterson books recommended in Chapter 1 (*Web Analytics Demystified* and *The Big Book of Key Performance Indicators*).

---

1. Halvorson, *Content Strategy for the Web*, 89.
2. The long URL: http://en.wikipedia.org/wiki/Turboencabulator

IN CONCLUSION

I began the first section of this book by noting that our discipline has no playbook from which "content strategies" can be selected. Which is too bad, because that would be much easier. What we have instead is a collection of principles, goals, approaches, and tools.

It might be useful to think of these pieces as the axons and synapses and other physical structures of the brain. The chemical and electrical impulses that make up our thoughts zoom along and hop between these structures; they aren't the structures themselves. In the same way, the values, approaches, and processes in this book are not "content strategy." Content strategy is what happens in the spaces between.

Where we're headed

Ten years ago, most "content" was either published using traditional print communication processes, or created by web writing pioneers and the first generation of specialist web editors.

Today, a slippage has unsettled these categories. Content is published on the web, in print, across multi-channel social networking systems, and in smartphone applications. And it's made and managed by people from a very wide range of backgrounds, from copywriters to data wranglers.

I predict that as the ways in which we communicate continue to evolve, the distinction between organizational communication strategy, company-wide information management, and content strategy will blur and disappear. And as this happens, our processes and tools will necessarily evolve to meet the changing needs of our clients and to serve the new shape of content itself. And from here, we can't quite see what that will mean.

If you're reading this book, you're probably part of that uncertain future. And you'll probably live through more than a few more gold rushes and subsequent periods of disenchantment. But no matter what happens around us, and no matter what challenges we're called to answer in the coming decades, a few things are constant. Those constants are the things that this book—and especially its first two sections—are meant to help nail down.

The better we understand the principles that underlie our work, the better prepared we'll be to advocate for content and its readers, long after the robot maids and flying cars finally come to lead us into the new world.

BONUS TRACK: SO HOW DO I GET IN?

Here's a little secret about content strategy: very few people got here on purpose. We mostly wandered in from one related field or another, found ourselves unable to stop fiddling with bad content, and decided to stick around and try to make things better. For people who want to begin doing content strategy work, this has good and bad implications. On the good side, it means that there are many paths into the field. On the bad side, it means that there is no single clear path.

Paradoxically, the best way to "get into content strategy" is to begin doing content strategy, whatever your job description currently is. Let's say you're interested in working as a content strategist, but you haven't worked much with web content. If you have experience in any of the sibling fields, your skills will almost certainly be relevant, and you'll probably want to spend some time boning up on at least two of the other areas. Content strategy is still sufficiently young that very few people working as content strategists now began their careers in the discipline; for most people, the move into CS work will either be lateral, from an equivalent position in a related discipline, or an expansion into CS from a more junior writing, editorial, design, or project coordination role.

No matter where you come from, a few characteristics seem to be requisite. You can't be ambivalent about the web. You might hate it sometimes, but it has to be in your blood. You have to care about getting things right, while understanding that "right" is something that constantly changes. You have to be reasonably good with people and exceptionally good at high-speed synthesis and pattern recognition. You need to have a solid grasp of the basics of information architecture. You need to care about design and front-end programming, which means you need to know enough about both to be able to care.

Oh, and you can't be humorless. I'm not sure why, but it doesn't work if you are.

Mars needs content strategists

If this sounds like your world and you have related skills, the easiest path is usually to begin taking work that's closer to what you want to do, and demonstrating along the way that you can do it. If you're not working in the web industry, start scooting toward the web side of your industry. If you're fresh out of school and want to work your way toward content strategy, seek web editorial, online marketing, web generalist, and information management experience.

Content strategy is an extremely friendly and talkative discipline. If you start by checking out the conversation that takes place on content blogs, attending conferences and meet-ups, and reading content strategy books and magazine articles, you'll probably get a pretty good idea of how you might make your way into the field. The truth is, we need you—there's more work here than we can do alone. Come say hi.

ACKNOWLEDGEMENTS

Thanks to the brilliant crew at A Book Apart for inviting me to write this book and seeing it through to the end:

To Jeffrey, for being a champion of that which is right and true in the world of web-making, and for giving me a series of much-needed shoves.

To Jason, for being the most inspiring designer a text nerd could hope to work with, and an inspiring advocate for content.

To Krista, for being a wonderful copyeditor and a great force for good in web publishing.

And especially to Mandy, for the superb edit and all the unflappable, steady-eyed support.

This book could not have happened without the extraordinarily generous people who make up the content strategy community and its advocates in other fields. The work of Kristina Halvorson and Melissa Rach of Brain Traffic has been absolutely foundational, and I also owe a debt to Ian Alexander, Rick Allen, Relly Annett-Baker, Rahel Anne Bailie, Margot Bloomstein, James Callan, Meghan Casey, Liz Danzico, Daniel Eizans, Paul Ford, Clinton Forry, Adam Greenfield, Matt Grocki, Dervala Hanley, Whitney Hess, Richard Ingram, Robert K. Jenkins III, Nicole Jones, Jonathan Kahn, Rachel Lovinger, Jeffrey MacIntyre, Karen McGrane, Elizabeth McGuane, Tim Meaney, Craig Mod, Elizabeth Schlatter, Randall Snare, Carolyn Wood, Rich Ziade, and the people I've forgotten, unforgivably, to list.

I owe special thanks to Colleen Jones and Tiffani Jones Brown for their careful reading and wise advice, and to Robert, Athena, and Wil for being born.

And thanks beyond thanks to PJ, for reading one million drafts, talking me down from the highest bookshelf, and making my life *so much fun.*

RESOURCES

This section lists books and major community websites. It does not include the dozens of blogs, blog posts, and online magazine articles I referred to while writing this book, and that I recommend to readers. Links need care and feeding, so they're best kept online where they can be maintained. You can find them, arranged by topic, at http://incisive.nu/elements.

Content Strategy: Basics, Tools, Techniques

If you're thinking of giving content strategy a shot, don't try to pick which of the following to read and bookmark. Start with Halvorson and Jones, and read on from there.

Ann Handley and C.C. Chapman, *Content Rules: How to Create Killer Blogs, Podcasts, Videos, Ebooks, Webinars (and More) That Engage Customers and Ignite Your Business*, (Hoboken: John Wiley and Sons, 2011).

Kristina Halvorson, *Content Strategy for the Web*, (California: New Riders, 2009).

Colleen Jones, *Clout: The Art and Science of Influential Web Content*, (California: New Riders, 2011).

Ann Rockley, *Managing Enterprise Content: A Unified Content Strategy*, (California: New Riders, 2003).

Richard Sheffield, *The Web Content Strategist's Bible*, (Georgia: CLUEfox Publishing, 2009).

A List Apart magazine, content strategy section: http://alistapart.com/topics/content/content-strategy/

Content Strategy Knol: http://knol.google.com/k/content-strategy

Google Groups Content Strategy Group: http://groups.google.
com/group/contentstrategy/ .

Essential Cross-Training

If you plan to work on the web, you need to understand the
disciplines that work together to make websites. These clas-
sics will get you up to speed.

Dan M. Brown, *Communicating Design: Developing Web Site
Documentation for Design and Planning*, Second Edition,
(California: New Riders, 2010).

Jesse James Garrett, *The Elements of User Experience: User-
Centered Design for the Web and Beyond*, Second Edition,
(California: New Riders, 2010).

Steve Krug, *Don't Make Me Think: A Common Sense Approach to
Web Usability*, Second Edition, (California: New Riders, 2005).

Peter Morville and Louis Rosenfeld, *Information Architecture
for the World Wide Web: Designing Large-Scale Web Sites*, Second
Edition, (Massachusetts: O'Reilly Media, 2006).

Janice (Ginny) Redish, *Letting Go of the Words: Writing Web
Content that Works*, (San Francisco: Morgan Kaufmann, 2007).

Jeffrey Zeldman with Ethan Marcotte, *Designing with Web
Standards*, Third Edition, (California: New Riders, 2009).

Influences: Editorial

The essence of editorial work lies not in style guides and arguments about grammar, but in the ability to cultivate relationships, manage chaos, and serve readers. It's not a profession to be learned from books, but these three very different takes will help.

Leonard S. Marcus, *Dear Genius: The Letters of Ursula Nordstrom*, (New York: HarperCollins, 2000).

Arthur Plotnik, *The Elements of Editing*, (New York: Collier Books, 1982).

William Strunk, Jr., and E.B. White, eds., *The Elements of Style*, Fourth Edition, (New York: Longman, 1999). Also excellent is the original full text of Strunk's 1918 edition online at: http://en.wikisource.org/wiki/The_Elements_of_Style

Influences: Curatorial

Museum workers have much to teach anyone who cares for stores of valuable information or seeks to educate, intrigue, and enlighten. From practice to theory, these texts will give you a peek into the curatorial world.

Bettina Carbonell, ed., *Museum Studies: An Anthology of Contexts*, (Massachusetts: Wiley-Blackwell, 2003).

James Cuno, *Whose Muse?: Art Museums and the Public Trust*, (Princeton: Princeton University Press, 2006).

Nina Simon, *The Participatory Museum*, (Museum 2.0, 2010). Full text online at http://participatorymuseum.org/

Influences: Marketing and Rhetoric

Many content strategy books, articles, and posts assume the need for persuasion. For a more hardcore approach and a consideration of the ethics and principles of rhetoric, try these starting points.

Patricia Bizzell, *The Rhetorical Tradition: Readings from Classical Times to the Present,* (New York: Bedford/St. Martin's, 2000).

James Conger, *The Necessary Art of Persuasion,* (Massachusetts: Harvard Business School Press, 2008). Full text available online at http://annbadillo.com/leadership/files/necessary_art_persuasion_jay_conger.pdf

Influences: Information Science

Taken in addition to the information architecture primers listed under Essential Cross-Training, these texts and sites offer a glimpse at the weird and interesting things happening at the intersection of content and technology.

Ann Rockley, Steve Manning, and Charles Cooper, *DITA 101: Fundamentals of DITA for Authors and Managers,* Second Edition, (Ontario: The Rockley Group, Inc., 2010)

DITA XML.org: http://dita.xml.org/

International Journal of Digital Curation: http://ijdc.net/index.php/ijdc

The Digital Curation Centre: http://www.dcc.ac.uk/

INDEX

Q

qualitative audit 53

R

Rach, Melissa 49
RFP 48–49
rhetoric 28, 30

S

Scher, Paula 16
SEO 15
sitemap 58, 62
stakeholders 49–50
storytelling 18-20
style guide 41, 44, 60, 61, 68
success metrics 41, 44, 50

T

taxonomies 34, 36, 39, 41
The Elements of Editing 18
traffic analysis 11, 40, 41, 44, 54, 69
Turing, Alan 16

U

user advocate 47-48
user-centered 8-9
user proxies 35, 47, 52
user research 11, 34, 42, 44, 47, 51,
     52, 58

W

Web Analytics Demystified 32, 70
webmaster 28, 35, 36
wireframes 35, 42, 58-61
WordPress 36
workflow 21, 36, 40-44, 54

Z

Zambonini, Dan 23

ABOUT A BOOK APART

Web design is about multi-disciplinary mastery and laser
focus, and that's the thinking behind our brief books for
people who make websites. We cover the emerging and
essential topics in web design and development with style,
clarity, and, above all, brevity—because working designer-
developers can't afford to waste time.

The goal of every title in our catalog is to shed clear light
on a tricky subject, and do it fast, so you can get back to work.
Thank you for supporting our mission to provide profession-
als with the tools they need to move the web forward.

COLOPHON

The text is set in FF Yoga and its companion, FF Yoga Sans,
both by Xavier Dupré. Headlines and cover are set in Titling
Gothic by David Berlow.

ABOUT THE AUTHOR

 Erin Kissane is a content strategist and editor based in New York City and Portland, Oregon. She was an editor at *A List Apart* magazine for nearly ten years, and has also been a freelance book editor and the editorial director of Happy Cog Studios. In 2011, she joined content strategy consultancy Brain Traffic, where she leads content projects and eats cake. When not working, Erin indulges her greed for books and coffee and writes about speculative and modernist fiction from the 1920s and 30s. She blogs at Incisive.nu.